Punks

Recent Titles in
Guides to Subcultures and Countercultures

The Ku Klux Klan: A Guide to an American Subculture
Martin Gitlin

Hippies: A Guide to an American Subculture
Micah L. Issitt

Guides to
Subcultures and
Countercultures

Punks:
A Guide to an American Subculture

Sharon M. Hannon

GREENWOOD PRESS

An Imprint of ABC-CLIO, LLC

A B C ☰ C L I O

Santa Barbara, California • Denver, Colorado • Oxford, England

Library of Congress Cataloging-in-Publication Data

Hannon, Sharon M.
  Punks : a guide to an American subculture / Sharon M. Hannon.
    p. cm. — (Guides to subcultures and countercultures)
  Includes bibliographical references and index.
    ISBN 978-0-313-36456-3 (hard copy : alk. paper) — ISBN 978-0-313-36457-0 (ebook)
  1. Punk rock music—Social aspects—United States. 2. Punk culture—United States. I. Title.
  ML3918.R63H35 2010
  306.4'8426—dc22   2009041377

14 13 12 11 10   1 2 3 4 5

This book is also available on the World Wide Web as an eBook.
Visit www.abc-clio.com for details.

Greenwood Press
An Imprint of ABC-CLIO, LLC

ABC-CLIO, LLC
130 Cremona Drive, P.O. Box 1911
Santa Barbara, California 93116-1911

This book is printed on acid-free paper ∞
Manufactured in the United States of America

This book is dedicated to Patti Smith,
who showed me that women have the right and ability to
look or sound any way they like. If they do their work with craft
and conviction, it will be respected.

Contents

Series Foreword

From beatniks to flappers, zoot-suiters to punks, this series brings to life some of the most compelling countercultures in American history. Designed to offer a quick, in-depth examination and current perspective on each group, the series aims to stimulate the reader's understanding of the richness of the American experience. Each book explores a countercultural group critical to American life and introduces the reader to its historical setting and precedents, the ways in which it was subversive or countercultural, and its significance and legacy in American history. Webster's Ninth New Collegiate Dictionary defines counterculture as "a culture with values and mores that run counter to those of established society." Although some of the groups covered can be described as primarily subcultural, they were targeted for inclusion because they have not existed in a vacuum. They have advocated for rules that methodically opposed mainstream culture or have lived by those ideals to the degree that it became impossible not to impact the society around them. They have left their marks, both positive and negative, on the fabric of American culture. Volumes cover such groups as hippies and beatniks, who impacted popular culture, literature, and art; eco-socialists and radical feminists, who worked toward social and political change; and even groups such as the Ku Klux Klan, who left mostly scars.

A lively alternative to narrow historiography and scholarly monographs, each volume in the *Guides to Subcultures and Countercultures* series can be described as a "library in a book," containing both essays and browseable reference materials, including primary documents, to enhance the research process and bring the content alive in a variety of ways. Written for students and general readers, each volume includes engaging illustrations, a timeline of critical events in the subculture, topical essays that illuminate aspects of the subculture, a glossary of subculture terms and slang, biographical sketches of the key players involved, and primary source excerpts—including speeches, writings, articles, first-person accounts, memoirs, diaries, government reports, and court decisions—that offer a contemporary perspective on each group. In addition, each volume includes an extensive bibliography of current recommended print and nonprint sources appropriate for further research.

Preface

Punk is personal. It means different things to different people. To me, as I listened to punk music and read about punk as a teenager, it represented freedom, new ideas, and the liberating realization that not everyone followed popular trends. It showed me that I had control over my life, that I could choose how I wanted to live. Punk music offered more than just great tunes I could jump around to. It opened up a world to me—full of intriguing, imaginative, diverse people trying to create art on their own terms and change American culture along the way.

In this book, I write about punk subculture in the United States, which began in New York City in the mid-1970s, has mutated many times, and continues in some fashion even today. I mention British punk culture wherever it had a great impact on American punk—something it did often in the early years.

This book examines punk subculture as expressed through music, fashion, and art. It also includes discussions about women in punk, about how mainstream media presented punk to the public, and about how punks came together through fanzines, clubs, radio stations, and record stores to develop their culture. Because punk has generated a large and unique vocabulary, a glossary of terms is also included.

As with any overview of punk, the essays and information in this book cannot encompass all of the various aspects of thirty-plus years of punk culture. The music, fanzines, record labels, and bands discussed provide an illustrative look at aspects of punk culture. Much more information about these topics and others can be found in the resources listed in the bibliography at the end of the book.

Every punk or former punk has a unique story, and this book includes several new interviews with people who were involved in the punk scenes in their communities. Their stories represent the stories of thousands of other punk fans who wrote fanzines, took photographs, formed bands, and started record labels.

As I talked to people and read what others have written about punk, one word came up over and over again: community. To many people, punk represented community much more than nihilism, epitomized empowerment and freedom more than anarchy or destruction.

With that in mind, I would like to thank the following people for making this book possible: Cynthia Connolly, Ian MacKaye, Loren Molinare, Jeff Nelson, and Steve Pick for sharing their stories with me; Angelina Keating, Susan Reyburn, Alan Bisbort, Heather Quinn, Stephanie Helline, Patti Tuohy, Heather Whyte, and Lisa White for their time and editorial and technical assistance; and Mark Rogovin, Athena Angelos, Tom Hearn, Lisa A. Hernandez, and Bert Queiroz for contributing photographs to this book. And I thank Jim Wyerman for his questions, suggestions, patience, and support.

Timeline of Punk Subculture

March 12, 1967	The Velvet Underground's debut album, *The Velvet Underground and Nico*, is released. Financed by Andy Warhol, it introduces Lou Reed to the world.
1969	Two Detroit originals, the MC5 and the Stooges, release their first albums, *Kick Out the Jams* and *The Stooges*.
1973	Tom Verlaine and Richard Hell form Television, one of the founding bands of the New York punk scene.
July 27, 1973	Protopunk band the New York Dolls release their self-titled debut.
December 10, 1973	Hilly Kristal opens a club, CBGBs, in an old derelict bar in New York City's Bowery neighborhood.
March 31, 1974	Television becomes the first "punk" band to play CBGBs. A few months later, the Ramones debut at the club.

March 1975	New York band the Dictators release their first album, *Go Girl Crazy*.
March 20, 1975	Television and Patti Smith begin a five-week residency at CBGBs. As a result, Smith is signed to a contract with Columbia Records.
July 16–August 2, 1975	CBGBs hosts the Festival of the Top 40 Unrecorded New York Rock Bands, featuring the Ramones, Television, Talking Heads, Blondie, the Heartbreakers, the Shirts, and others.
November 6, 1975	At St. Martin's School of Art in London, the Sex Pistols play their first show.
November 1975	Patti Smith's *Horses* is released on Arista Records, eventually reaching #47 on the U.S. charts.
January 1, 1976	John Holmstrom, Legs McNeil, and Ged Dunn publish the maiden issue of *Punk*, the first magazine to focus on the CBGBs music scene.
April 23, 1976	The Ramones debut, *Ramones*, is released on Sire Records.
July 4, 1976	In a watershed event for the London punk scene, the Ramones play the Roundhouse, in London, their first show outside the United States.
1977	Two influential California bands form: Black Flag in Hermosa Beach and the Germs in Los Angeles.
	Punk rock radio show Maximum Rocknroll begins broadcasting in the San Francisco Bay area.
	Punk store Manic Panic opens in New York City at 33 St. Mark's Place.
February 1977	The Weirdos form in Los Angeles.

Spring 1977	Filipino restaurant the Mabuhay Gardens emerges as San Francisco's premier punk rock club when rock promoter/television producer Dirk Dirksen begins regularly booking punk bands there.
May 1977	The first issue of the Los Angeles fanzine *Slash* is produced to chronicle the burgeoning local punk scene.
August 18, 1977	The Masque, the first Los Angeles club devoted to new bands and punk music, opens in a basement off Hollywood Boulevard.
August 28, 1977	*Flipside* fanzine, printed by graduates from Whittier High School in Southern California, debuts.
September 26, 1977	The Germs release their first single, "Forming," on What? Records.
October 28, 1977	The Sex Pistols release *Never Mind the Bollocks, Here's the Sex Pistols*. It reaches #1 in England and influences a generation of future American punks.
1978	Bob Biggs founds the Slash record label in Los Angeles, and Black Flag guitarist Greg Ginn forms SST Records in Hermosa Beach, California.
January 14, 1978	At San Francisco's Winterland ballroom, the Sex Pistols play their last show and break up. Local bands the Nuns and the Avengers open the show.
March 1978	The Dickies are signed by A&M Records, becoming the first—and only—early Los Angeles punk band signed by a major record label.
July 19, 1978	At San Francisco's Mabuhay Gardens, the Dead Kennedys play their first show. The

	following year they release their single "California Über Alles."
January 1979	Black Flag release their first record, the *Nervous Breakdown* EP, on SST.
February 1979	In a basement in Forestville, Maryland, Bad Brains play their first show.
February 2, 1979	Sex Pistol Sid Vicious dies of a heroin overdose, almost four months after his arrest for murdering his girlfriend in New York's Chelsea Hotel.
April 25, 1980	British band the Clash make their American television debut on *Fridays*, a weekly comedy show.
June 23, 1980	Bad Brains release their first single, *Pay to Cum*, considered the fastest music ever recorded to date.
June 29, 1980	The *Los Angeles Times* runs the first of many articles about violence at local punk concerts.
December 1980	Ian MacKaye and Jeff Nelson found Dischord Records in Washington, D.C., and release their first record, the Teen Idles' *Minor Disturbance* EP.
December 7, 1980	The Germs lead singer Darby Crash commits suicide at age twenty-two.
December 13, 1980	At their first show, Washington, D.C., hardcore band Minor Threat open for Bad Brains.
January 18, 1981	The Plasmatics' singer Wendy O. Williams is arrested in Milwaukee for onstage obscenity after she fondles a sledgehammer. The next night in Cleveland, she is arrested again on the same charge.
July 1, 1981	Filmmaker Penelope Spheeris' document of the Los Angeles punk scene, *The Decline of Western Civilization*, is released.

December 1981	With their new singer, Henry Rollins, Black Flag releases their first album, *Damaged*.
1982	Issue #0 of fanzine *Maximum Rocknroll* is published as a spinoff of the punk rock radio show.
January 1982	Television series *CHiPs* runs an episode featuring destructive punk characters. Several other shows, including *Quincy, M.E.*, will soon include punks in their storylines.
July 29, 1984	Rites of Spring, the Washington, D.C., band often credited with launching emocore, or emo, play their first show.
1987	Larry Livermore and David Hayes found Lookout! Records in Northern California to release music by San Francisco Bay area punk bands.
September 8, 1988	Epitaph records, founded by Brett Gurewitz and Greg Graffin, releases Bad Religion's influential album, *Suffer*.
1990	Fat Mike of NOFX starts the Fat Wreck Chords record label.
April 23, 1991	Guitarist Johnny Thunders of the New York Dolls and the Heartbreakers dies in New Orleans of an apparent methadone and alcohol overdose. He is thirty-eight.
Summer 1991	Female musicians and zine writers found Riot Grrrl in Washington, D.C.
August 20–25, 1991	The International Pop Underground (IPU) Convention is held in Olympia, Washington. Organized by K Records, the festival pulls together musicians (fifty bands in six days), independent label owners, and fans; launches the fiercely independent Kill Rock Stars label; and helps to jump-start the Riot Grrrl movement.

September 24, 1991   Nirvana releases its album *Nevermind*, which hits #1 on the U.S. charts and ushers in the grunge era.

February 1, 1994   Green Day puts our their third album, *Dookie*, which becomes one of the best-selling punk records of all time.

April 5, 1994   Kurt Cobain of Nirvana commits suicide. He is twenty-seven.

August 4, 1995   The first Warped Tour, a traveling festival showcasing punk rock and skateboarding contests, kicks off in Salt Lake City, Utah. Over the next decade, the tour becomes the longest-running traveling music festival in the world.

August 22, 1995   California band Rancid release their third album, . . . *And Out Come the Wolves*, which sells more than a million copies.

1996   Eighteen years after breaking up, the Sex Pistols reunite for a U.S. tour. In a bit of intentional irony, they call it *The Filthy Lucre Tour*.

May 25, 1996   Bradley Nowell, singer/guitarist for Sublime, dies from a heroin overdose, causing the band to break up. Nowell is twenty-eight.

April 15, 2001   Joey Ramone dies from lymphoma at age fifty. He will be followed by Dee Dee Ramone (June 5, 2002) and Johnny Ramone (September 15, 2004).

March 18, 2002   The Ramones become the first punk band inducted into the Rock and Roll Hall of Fame.

September 4, 2002   Inland Invasion 2002, the largest American punk concert ever, is held outside Los Angeles. An estimated 50,000 punk fans brave the desert heat and dust to see TSOL, the Adolescents, Social Distortion, the Sex Pistols, and others.

February 13, 2005	Green Day wins the Grammy Award for Best Rock Album for *American Idiot*.
October 15, 2006	Legendary punk club CBGBs closes due to financial difficulties.
June 2007	Influential zine *Punk Planet* ceases publication after thirteen years and eighty issues.
October 2009	*Maximum Rocknroll* puts out issue #317.

CHAPTER ONE | # What Is Punk?

[Punk] means anti-authority, independent, tricky, unsentimental, dirty, quick, subversive, guiltless. It means not accepting the ordinary terms of behavior. It also means resisting classification, which is a good paradox, since of course "punk" is a classification.[1]

—Richard Hell, the Voidoids

Punk means not being taken in by propaganda or spin. Being able to think for yourself and form your own opinions.[2]

—Joe Strummer, the Clash

So-called punk rock music and punk are really two very different things, and what I believe punk is to me is a belief I will live and breathe and carry till the day I die. Not self-destruction, but true love of oneself.[3]

—Danny Furious, the Avengers

Punk—one of the most discussed, analyzed, and written-about youth movements of the twentieth century—is elusive. There is no universally accepted definition of punk, particularly among those who consider themselves punk. To some, punk means rebellion against conformity or against parents, school, work, and society at large. To others it means taking control of your life and getting things done without waiting for someone to help you or approve your idea. And to others punk is a loud, fast style of music played with minimal ornamentation or production but a lot of heart and sincerity.

At one time, rock and roll also meant most of these same things, but by the time punk rock appeared in the 1970s, rock and roll had lost its edge. Punk sharpened the blade and sliced through the pompous, bloated pretentions of arena rock shows' thirty-minute songs and twenty-minute drum solos, offering audiences a refreshing authenticity and immediacy. It broke down the barriers that separated the audience from the musicians and even from each other and helped a new community to grow around two principles: individuality is paramount, and anyone can create great art. From the beginning, punks embraced the do-it-yourself (DIY) ethos, disregarded authority, and rejected corporate commercialism. These concepts inspired tens of thousands in the punk scene to create their own music, art, film, fashions, and writings and to engage in free thought, direct action, rebellion, and work to change the world.

Best-selling crime novelist George Pelecanos, for example, credits the early Washington, D.C., punk scene and bands such as Bad Brains and Minor Threat with giving him the courage to first start writing. As a young man and a punk fan, Pelecanos understood that punk band members didn't have to be musicians, didn't have to have ties to a record company, and didn't have to know someone important. Most just picked up an instrument and created something. For Pelecanos, his instrument would be a pen.

Punks' disregard for authority and capitalism led them to reject the predominant culture as hypocritical, shallow, and false. To them, that culture rewards conformity above all else; there is no room for the creative, the individual, or the different. With their focus on the individual, punks have no one cohesive political philosophy—some are apolitical, some would be considered progressives or anarchists, and some subsets have been known for their extreme racist, sexist, or homophobic views.

Origin of "Punk"

Rock critic Dave Marsh has been widely credited with coining the term "punk rock" in a review of the band ? and the Mysterians in a 1971 issue of *Creem*, an irreverent music magazine. Before then, a "punk" was a male hustler or criminal. Punk was more clearly described by Lenny Kaye, music writer and future guitarist for the Patti Smith Group, who used the term in his liner notes to the 1972 album *Nuggets: Original Artifacts from the First Psychedelic Era (1965–1968)*, a compilation of music from American psychedelic bands and garage one-hit wonders. The bands on *Nuggets* were, in Kaye's words, "young, decidedly unprofessional, seemingly more at home practicing for a teen dance than going out on national tour. The name that has been unofficially coined for them—punk rock—seems particularly fitting in this case."[4]

Several years later, when three young guys in New York City—Legs McNeil, John Holmstrom, and Ged Dunn—started a magazine focusing on the new bands playing at a downtown club called CBGBs, eighteen-year-old McNeil suggested they call it *Punk*. "The word 'punk' seemed to sum up the thread that connected everything we liked—drunk, obnoxious, smart but not pretentious, absurd, funny, ironic, and things that appealed to the darker side,"[5] he said. *Punk*, a homemade, hand-lettered, cartoon-filled fanzine debuted in January 1976, bringing DIY into the realm of publishing. Soon after, journalists applied the punk rock label to New York groups as diverse as the Ramones, Blondie, Patti Smith, the Dead Boys, and the Talking Heads. A movement was born.

Punk magazine creators John Holmstrom, Legs McNeil, and Ged Dunn in front of their headquarters, the "Punk Dump," in 1976. (© Tom Hearn. www.rumblegraphics.com. Used by permission.)

Writer John Rockwell wrote in 1977: ". . . by any logical criterion, the current New York rock scene is a movement. The movement is defined first of all on a social level: the bands know one another, steal members from one another, and hang out in the same clubs. Second, they share a common lineage, from the Velvet Underground through the [New York] Dolls to Patti Smith. And third, the very act of being perceived as a group from without establishes them as such."[6]

> The idea of punk that I liked was that you don't have to be an expert. An amateur is a good thing. An amateur is somebody who does something because they like doing it . . . You can try different things. You could try going on-stage before you were a virtuoso. You could pick up a camera if you hadn't gone to photography school.[7]
> —Roberta Bayley, photographer

Most of the early New York punk bands sounded nothing alike. Some were still learning to play their instruments and write their first songs, but to their audience it didn't matter how well they played. The point was that they were playing what they wanted to play, not what they thought would be commercially successful.

> People [were] bored with [self-]indulgent musicianship. Things were getting very stale in the music business; records were very beautifully produced, with beautiful precision, like one backing track would take two days to get down in the studio. But now there's a new approach which is: ENERGY, ENJOYMENT, FEELING—an EMOTIONAL thing, really. There's definitely a big difference in approach and you can hear it.
> —V. Vale, founder *Search and Destroy* fanzine, 1977[8]

By early 1977, punk exploded in London, inspired in part by American bands, including the New York Dolls and the Ramones, but imbued with a sense of political and social purpose and a more extreme style. In Great Britain, the late 1970s was a time of great unemployment and social unrest, when underprivileged white working-class kids felt alienated from British culture, foreseeing their lives with few prospects and "no future" as the Sex Pistols famously sang in their nihilist masterpiece "God Save the Queen." A new crop of bands and their fans crudely questioned authority and the very basics of the culture: God, country, work, society, race, and sex. Unlike previous subcultures, British punks deliberately cultivated a violent, deviant, disgusting image. As a result, most Americans first learned about punk through sensationalized newscasts about the antics of the Sex Pistols and their fans, who pierced their cheeks with safety pins, wore ripped clothing, vomited in public, and cursed on television.

Unlike in Great Britain, the first punk scenes that developed in U.S. cities were initiated by young people in two distinct groups: (1) art students who fancied themselves poets, writers, filmmakers, and painters and (2) middle-class kids from the suburbs who saw punk as a way to express their frustrations and discontent with the world. In almost every major city, these two groups coexisted uneasily, and each supported the bands that more closely reflected their personal sensibilities, be it Television and the Ramones in New York, the Screamers and the Germs in Los Angeles, or Crime and the Nuns in San Francisco.

DID YOU KNOW?

Punk Names
Jan Paul Beahm (Darby Crash)
Eric Boucher (Jello Biafra)
John Genzale, Jr. (Johnny Thunders)
David Xavier Harrigan (Tomata du Plenty)
Johnny Madansky (Johnny Blitz)
Richard Meyers (Richard Hell)
Tom Miller (Tom Verlaine)
Gene O'Connor (Cheetah Chrome)
Danny O'Brien (Danny Furious)
Simon John Ritchie (Sid Vicious)

Taking a page from earlier art movements such as the Dadaists and the Futurists, as well as the British punks, American punks chose to be subversive, shock by their appearance, reject established social norms, and attempt to break down the standard barriers between audiences and performers. Punk shows were exercises in engagement. Rather than idolize bands, some punks spit on the groups or threw bottles or cans at them—but most just danced. "Once you stand a few feet from Dee Dee Ramone at a club in Falls Church, Virginia, you know you're not going back to the arena any time soon, if ever," said Henry Rollins, former singer for Black Flag.[9]

Hardcore

> I think one of the most important chapters in the history of rock and roll, the history of music, was the time that all the kids got together and wrote their own songs, formed their own bands, put on their own shows, put out their own records, made their own magazines, set up their own touring networks. [10]
>
> —Ian MacKaye, Minor Threat, Fugazi

As many in the first wave of punk rockers left the punk scene, found commercial success that drew them far from their roots, or died, a new punk scene erupted in the late 1970s. The songs were furiously fast, the dancing increasingly dangerous, and the crowds younger than earlier American punks. Art students no longer guided the look and fashion— suburban white males in jeans, T-shirts, hooded sweatshirts, and work boots or Chuck Taylor tennis shoes were firmly at the forefront of this scene, replacing the dyed hair, Mohawks, and safety pins favored by earlier punks. This new demographic also included skateboarders, surfers, BMX bikers, and graffiti writers, each of whom influenced the scene. Their music would come to be called hardcore, after a term believed to have been coined in 1981 by the Vancouver band DOA for their Hardcore 81 show. To the people in the scene, hardcore meant they were the real punks—the real deal. Few were influenced by any New York punk bands other than the Ramones, who were admired for their simplicity and speed. Hardcore was loud, fast, aggressive, and sounded like nothing that had come before. There was no singing, per se—vocalists screamed lyrics expressing the bands' anger and their disdain for mainstream America. Hardcore owed no debt to rock and roll or the blues.

Hardcore's rise coincided with the Reagan revolution and difficult economic times. As artist Winston Smith remembers, "Ronald Reagan was a catalyst for the hardcore scene."[11] With the country in a recession, plagued by high inflation and unemployment, the bands, full of disaffected young white men, seemed united in their opposition to Reagan. To these kids, many from broken families, the American dream was elusive. They were angry. For them, it was not the "morning in America" that Reagan had promised.

The bands and their fans realized there was no money to be made or careers to be had from playing hardcore. They were part of a subculture in which the general public had no interest. They did what they did because they loved it and, as a result, they were in charge of their entire scene. If they wanted to tour, they had to arrange it themselves, traveling by van and sleeping on friends' floors. If they wanted to record, they paid for it themselves, creating their own record labels, advertising their records in fanzines (called zines [pronounced *zeens*] for short) and mailing them to buyers. Mike Watt, bassist for 1980s band the Minutemen, remembers, "Punk was about more than just starting a band. It was about starting a label, it was about touring, it was about taking control. It was like songwriting; you just do it. You want a record, you pay the pressing plant. That's what it was all about."[12]

Hardcore punks constantly battled the police and authorities, particularly in Southern California, where the scene was huge and the police

A punk poses in his room in Buffalo, New York, in 1991. Note the circled-A anarchy symbol on the wall. (Library of Congress, Prints & Photographs Div., photograph © Milton Rogovin, 1952–2002, Punks series, 1991. [Repro #LC-RG15-VII-53] Used by permission of the Rogovin Collection, LLC.)

Two punks at home in Buffalo, New York, in 1991. (Library of Congress, Prints & Photographs Div., photograph © Milton Rogovin, 1952–2002, Punks series, 1991. [Repro #LC-RG15-VII-44] Used by permission of the Rogovin Collection, LLC.)

had a reputation for excessive violence. Media reports about the violence only served to attract new hardcore punks to the scene—punks with as much interest in brawling as in the music. As the violence escalated, it eventually alienated many older musicians and fans. By 1986, most of the original hardcore bands had broken up or changed direction.

Straight Edge

In the early 1980s, the mainstream media associated punk with nihilism and Sex Pistol Sid Vicious, who had died of a drug overdose in

February 1979, just months after being arrested for killing his girlfriend. Certainly a lot of punks drank excessively and used drugs, particularly in the brutally violent hardcore scene that developed in Orange County, California. But some hardcore bands took the opposite approach and adopted a straight-edge lifestyle that eschewed drinking, smoking, and even indiscriminate sex (although the latter was the least promoted aspect of straight edge). The term "straight edge" came from a 1981 song written by Ian MacKaye, then singer for hardcore band Minor Threat. MacKaye, who believed his sobriety gave him a mental and physical advantage over those who put their energy into sex, drugs, and alcohol, wrote the songs "Out of Step" and "Straight Edge" to explain how he lived his life. His attitude struck a chord with some kids and bands that adopted a sober lifestyle and then started the straight-edge movement. In Boston and New York, SS Decontrol (SSD) and Youth of Today enforced strict straight-edge rules at their shows. In time, attitudes devolved to the point of violence as straight-edge adherents attacked people who were drunk or on drugs. Claiming that he never intended to start a movement or tell others how to behave, MacKaye distanced himself from the movement as it grew more intolerant and extreme in the late 1980s.

Subcultures within a Subculture

After hardcore, the term "punk" fell out of favor for a time as former punk bands, such as Hüsker Dü, suddenly found themselves labeled "alternative" or "indie" (for independent) in the music press. While existing punk scenes fractured into smaller scenes with varying musical styles, other small groups of punks carved out their own niche in the world, places where they could truly live outside mainstream America.

In the punk universe, gutter punks live on the farthest edges of mainstream society usually on the streets or in abandoned buildings. They tend to travel in small groups, have no income, and survive from day to day by begging and panhandling. Many of these young punks started as runaways and, having survived difficult childhoods, choose to live their lives on the fringes of society rather than join the system that brutalized them.

Anarchy has been a popular political stance for punks since the Sex Pistols released their first record, "Anarchy in the U.K.," in 1976.

Although numerous bands have placed anarchy's circled A logo on their flyers and albums, for many it has been more of a viewpoint than a lifestyle. But, for true anarcho-punks, the British anarchist band Crass, active from 1978 to 1984, set the first example of anarchy as political and social action. Crass lived communally and strictly adhered to the DIY ethic. They engaged in civil disobedience, performed most shows to benefit causes such as squatter rights, and actively supported feminism, pacifism, animal rights, and other causes. Crass had enormous influence on future punks who sought ways to use direct action to affect change in society, particularly in Great Britain, and among some hardcore bands such as MDC from Austin, Texas.

Diversity in Punk

The early 1990s was a time of transition and change as activists started their own movements to confront the sexist or homophobic attitudes they had witnessed within punk culture. Openly gay people had always participated in punk, particularly in larger cities. Even in the hyper-masculine hardcore scene, there were several openly gay bands, including MDC and Big Boys. By the mid-1980s, the term "homocore" was first used to describe gay participation in punk, and a number of zines sprang up to give gay punks a forum. Within a few years, high-profile "queercore" bands started to emerge—Team Dresch, Tribe 8, and Pansy Division—that were open and confrontational about their sexuality. As the queercore movement grew, the music became more diversified. The bands, which first released their music on their own labels such as Chainsaw or Candy Ass Records, were soon working with larger independent labels. Homo a Go Go in Olympia, Washington, and other festivals were eventually established to showcase queer zines, films, music, and bands and, by the late 1990s, a strong gay presence was acknowledged, if not always accepted, by punks.

During the hardcore years, many women felt alienated from punk, leading them to create feminist punk zines and bands. In 1991, a group of women in Washington, D.C., including women in the bands Bikini Kill and Bratmobile, began a series of meetings that led to the Riot Grrrl movement, which sought to empower women in punk to take charge and create their own art and cultural material. The movement quickly spread across the country and overseas as confident and assertive young women examined and changed their roles within the punk scene.

The 1990s also saw an increase in the number of punks adopting a vegetarian or vegan lifestyle. To some, vegetarianism/veganism was a natural expansion of their straight-edge lifestyle. Others believed that animals should not be exploited for capitalist gains, and still others chose to do as little harm as possible to the environment. Some well-known punk vegetarians, such as Fat Mike from NOFX and Ian MacKaye, also helped to inform punks how they could support their basic principles through their lifestyles.

But the change that had the biggest impact on punk in the 1990s was punk rock's sudden acceptance by mainstream culture after the band Nirvana released their multi-million-selling album *Nevermind* in 1991. A new breed of punk-sounding bands emerged, and their willingness to accept corporate sponsorship and money from major record labels ignited a firestorm of controversy within the punk scene about the core issue of what it means to be punk. And as with most things punk, there is no universal agreement.

What is clear in the new century is that punk has had a dramatic impact on mainstream American culture by invigorating local music scenes, empowering young people to share their opinions through zines and later blogs, and initiating a DIY approach to life that has been subsumed in mainstream culture. Everywhere people routinely film and edit their own movies, record and release their own music, promote themselves on the Internet and through social networking sites, and write and publish their own books. Writers, filmmakers, advertising executives, and graphic artists who grew up influenced by punk routinely incorporate aspects of punk music and art into their work. As photographer Cynthia Connolly notes, "Now you can't even discern punk culture from the mainstream. So much of punk culture is enveloped in our American culture that it is our American culture."[13]

NOTES

1. Hell, Richard. "My Punk Beginnings & Are Rock Lyrics Poetry?" *Richard Hell Official Site*, www.richardhell.com/punkpoetry.html.
2. *Let's Rock Again*, DVD extras, directed by Dick Rude, 2004.

3. Academic Computer Club Umea University, "Danny Furious of the Avengers Interviewed," www.acc.umu.se/~samhain/summerofhate/avengersinterview.html.
4. Kaye, Lenny. *Nuggets*, ©1976, Sire Records, back cover text.
5. McNeil, Legs, and Gillian McCain. *Please Kill Me* (New York: Penguin Books, 1996), 204.
6. Rockwell, John. "Underground Rock Rises to the Surface . . . via Television," *Chicago Tribune*, April 1, 1977, E20.
7. Robinson, Charlotte. "She Just Takes Pictures—Interview with Roberta Bayley," August 30, 2000, *PopMatters*, www.popmatters.com/music/features/000830 -bayley.html.
8. Vale, V. "What Is Punk Rock and How Did It Begin?" *Researchpubs.com*, www.researchpubs.com/features/whatispunk.php.
9. *Punk's Not Dead*, directed by Susan Dynner, 2007.
10. Ibid.
11. Blush, Steven. *American Hardcore* (Los Angeles: Feral House, 2001), 20.
12. Azerrad, Michael. *Our Band Could Be Your Life* (Boston, New York, London: Little, Brown and Company, 2001), 6.
13. Interview with the author, January 17, 2009.

| # Punk Rock

The roots of punk rock lead directly back to the protopunk bands, the musicians from the 1960s and early 1970s who are most often credited with influencing the sound and attitude of basic punk rock. Although many of these protopunk bands sounded nothing like each other, they all shared two traits: the belief that they didn't have to be musical virtuosos to make good music and a defiant "we play what we want" attitude. These two ideas would remain at the core of what many people thought, think, of as punk rock.

Rebellious, rudimentary musicians were common in rock and roll from 1950s-era rebels such as Gene Vincent to the young Rolling Stones and the 1960s garage bands the Seeds and the Standells. As rock music began to grow increasingly complex after 1965, protopunks continued to play the music they liked rather than cater to the tastes of the general public, who soon grew accustomed to complex harmonies, synthesizers, and intricate multi-tracked guitar and keyboard parts. For example, in 1972, British progressive rock band Pink Floyd spent seven months recording *The Dark Side of the Moon*. By contrast, the Stooges recorded their first album in two days. The Ramones spent less than a week recording their debut. It's not that the punks didn't care about what they played—they simply understood that energy and authenticity can make a song more compelling than a ten-minute guitar solo from a music school graduate.

New York City's Velvet Underground, who recorded their first album in 1966 during the height of flower power, is often considered one of the first protopunk bands. With Lou Reed's songs about drugs and sadomasochism, the band, featuring John Cale on electric viola, were so different from bands played on the radio that they sounded as if they had arrived from another planet. They were so far ahead of their time that their first two albums still sound contemporary today.

Playing a ferocious style of in-your-face rock, the MC5 (Motor City 5) from Detroit inspired countless young musicians to pick up a guitar and wail. That the band actually could play their instruments may have relegated them to the sidelines in some punk histories in favor of Michigan's more primitive band, the Stooges, with their ultimate punk singer, Iggy Pop. But both bands were incredibly influential. Says Loren Molinare, guitarist for the Dogs, who formed in Lansing, Michigan, in 1968, "If you grew up in Michigan, it was Michigan rock first. In 1967, early 1968 it was the MC5 and the White Panthers and the whole Detroit scene was just booming."[1]

SOME INFLUENTIAL PUNK ALBUMS

Horses	Patti Smith (1975)
Ramones	Ramones (1976)
Fresh Fruit for Rotting Vegetables	Dead Kennedys (1980)
Damaged	Black Flag (1981)
Bad Brains	Bad Brains (1982)
Double Nickels on the Dime	Minutemen (1984)
Zen Arcade	Hüsker Dü (1984)
Suffer	Bad Religion (1988)
Complete Discography	Minor Threat (1989)
Operation Ivy	Operation Ivy (1991)

The First Wave of American Punk: New York City

At the beginning of 1974, the New York City rock scene could be summed up in three words: New York Dolls. With their souped-up R&B and 1960s-era girl group background vocals, the Dolls were the campy heroes of New York rock and just about the only thing happening in the city. Like every other protopunk band, they never sold many records, but they greatly influenced the few people who bought them.

Just as the Dolls' career began sputtering to an end, a new music scene was beginning in downtown Manhattan, where Hilly Kristal started booking a wide range of local bands into his club CBGB-OMFUG (Country, Bluegrass, Blues, and Other Music for Uplifting Gourmandizers), later known as CBGBs. Television, the Patti Smith Group, and the Talking Heads were led by writer/artist/musicians with college educations and art school backgrounds, while others like the Dictators, the Ramones, the Heartbreakers, and the Dead Boys featured gritty street kids voicing male teenage angst and obsessions: girls, cars, and partying. Others, such as Blondie with their early 1960s girl-group pop, and Suicide, which offered a moody, threatening form of early electronica, also found a place in the downtown scene. The only thread that connected these bands at first was that they wrote their own music, which was Kristal's initial criteria for allowing a band to play at his club. As John Holmstrom, cofounder of *Punk* magazine, described the scene in 1976, "there were only two authentic punk rock bands in New York at the time, the Ramones and the Dictators, and most of the kids who hung out at CBGBs were just an assortment of college kids, hippies, ex-glam rockers, and weirdos. Not a single punk among them."[2]

Television was the first new band to perform their own music at CBGBs, debuting there on March 31, 1974. Founded by Tom Verlaine (guitar) and Richard Hell (bass) in 1973, Television played fairly long songs with soaring, melodic solos by guitarist Richard Lloyd, who wove his notes in and out of Verlaine's jagged, sharp guitar lines. Their musical improvisations were in many ways closer to jazz than to most of the music later classified as punk. Despite Television's rough edges, Kristal invited them back to perform with the Ramones, four working-class kids from the Queens borough of New York City. It was the Ramones and their sound (raw, fast, and loud) and songs (short) that paved the way for the punk bands of the future. Without poetry or pretense, these four guys, dressed in black leather jackets, ripped blue jeans, and sneakers, slammed out "Blitzkrieg Bop," "Beat on the Brat," and "Cretin Hop." That Television and the Ramones performed on the same bill illustrates Kristal's somewhat haphazard approach to booking bands as he found out about them.

After the weight of egos, addiction, and poor record sales caused the New York Dolls to implode in 1975, Richard Hell left Television to form the Heartbreakers with the Dolls' Johnny Thunders (guitar)

The Ramones—Johnny, Tommy, Joey, and Dee Dee—backstage in New Haven, Connecticut, in 1976. (© Tom Hearn. www.rumblegraphics.com. Used by permission.)

and Jerry Nolan (drums). Hell, described by future Sex Pistols manager Malcolm McLaren as "a wonderful, bored, drained, scarred, dirty guy with a torn T-shirt,"[3] is credited with popularizing the first punk look—short spiky hair and ripped clothing held together with safety pins. Within a year, Hell left the Heartbreakers to form his own band, the Voidoids.

Meanwhile Patti Smith had been reading her poetry to Lenny Kaye's guitar accompaniment for several years and was making a name for herself writing for *Creem*, *Rolling Stone*, and *Crawdaddy* when she debuted at CBGBs with her full rock and roll band. "The band was great, Patti was great; every show was special," Kristal said. "Their audiences, because of [the band's] notoriety, were composed of writers, artists, musicians, and other celebrities (all fans). It was a most unusual crowd ranging from punks to professors."[4] Kristal signed Smith to do a seven-week residency that saw her audience and status grow, culminating in a record contract with Arista Records.

With new bands springing up by the hour, CBGBs hosted the Festival of the Top 40 Unrecorded New York Rock Bands in the summer of 1975, featuring the Ramones, Television, Talking Heads, Blondie, the

the Heartbreakers, the Shirts, and others. Within another year, the best of these bands had record deals, outgrew CBGBs, and left New York to tour. New bands, including the Dead Boys, who moved to New York from Ohio in 1976, kept things lively for a while, but by 1978, four years after Television played their first show at the club, the initial CBGBs scene was over. By that time, the media and music industry's attention was focused on London's more visually extreme and musically consistent punk scene, led by the Sex Pistols, the Damned, and the Clash.

The First Wave of American Punk: San Francisco

In early 1976, San Francisco had no place where unknown local rock bands could play, but that changed as word slowly seeped out about the punk scene in New York. National magazines *Rock Scene* and *Hit Parader* had already run stories about Patti Smith, Television, and the Ramones, and Smith had performed twice in Berkeley by late 1975. But in August 1976, the Ramones played the Savoy Tivoli Theater— a show that left a great impression on the few people who attended, including V. Vale, founder of *Search and Destroy*, the first Bay-area zine. "There was all this contrivance and artiness in rock music," he wrote, "and the Ramones brought in a blast of something totally opposite, minimalist, just really intense and driving with all the fat trimmed away. Twenty songs in twenty minutes."[5]

During this same time, artists, students, and musicians such as Jeff Olener and Tommy Gear visited New York and returned west, inspired by what they had seen at CBGBs. One of San Francisco's first punk groups soon grew out of a movie project by Olener and fellow film student Alejandro Escovedo. Needing a band for their film project but lacking money to pay one, they cast themselves and wrote a few songs. From this inauspicious beginning the Nuns arose. In late 1976, Olener convinced Ness Aquino, owner of the Mabuhay Gardens, to let the band play at his club. When they drew a decent crowd, Aquino agreed to book other bands, though few realized that this combination of punk and the "Fab Mab," as the venue was later known, would become the magnet that would draw together the artists, photographers, musicians, and writers who would make up the San Francisco punk scene. The next year, the Nuns added singer Jennifer Miro and built a large local following. Beatnik poet Allen Ginsberg saw them at the time and commented, "I like the Nuns. They're like Kabuki Theater. I've been to CBGBs 15 or 20 times but now I think the Mabuhay is a better scene. CBGBs is a bit tired." [6] When the Sex Pistols came to the city in January 1978 for the last show of their ill-fated U.S. tour, the Nuns and the Avengers, another local band, opened the show, performing for more than 5,000 people.

In January 1977, Crime, created by former glam rock guitarists/ singers Johnny Strike and Frankie Fix, played their first show at the Mabuhay. With their slicked-back hair and songs that sounded like revved up, distorted Chuck Berry tunes, Crime clearly illustrated punk's connection to early rock and roll. The band quickly recorded and self-released a single, "Hot Wire My Heart," backed with "Baby You're So Repulsive," said to be the first record released by a West Coast punk band.

A third key San Francisco band, the Avengers, were formed in 1976 by art students Danny Furious and Greg Ingraham, who enlisted another student, nineteen-year-old Penelope Houston, as their singer. Early on, the group focused on writing and performing original material and, in 1977, Dangerhouse Records released the group's three-song EP (extended play 7-inch single). Although the record received enthusiastic reviews and sold well, larger record labels were not interested in the Avengers, or any other San Francisco bands.

Throughout 1977, the Damned, Devo, the Ramones, Blondie, and other bands traveling to San Francisco played the Mabuhay alongside the ever-expanding legion of homegrown bands including UXA, Sleeper, Negative Trend, and Grand Mal. By the time of the Sex Pistols' 1978 breakup, the audience at punk shows had started to change, with fans aping the more extreme dress and dance styles of British punk. According to Avenger Jimmy Wilsey, his band broke up "when cops started beating up people at shows" [7] as the music turned toward hardcore and the scene became more violent.

The First Wave of American Punk: Hollywood

Local bands in Los Angeles had the same problems as their brethren in other cities. The few clubs that featured live rock music, the Whisky and the Starwood, only booked bands that had record contracts. When the Dogs, an unsigned band from Michigan, moved to Los Angeles in April 1975, they found they couldn't get a gig.

Says Loren Molinare, the Dogs' guitarist:

We met the Motels and the Pop and started the Radio Free Hollywood coalition out of a necessity to band together against "the man" or the Hollywood mafia, as we called them. We had a friend at the Los Angeles City Parks and he let us do shows at Griffith Park. Then we did a show at Trouper's Hall at LaBrea and Hollywood Boulevard, which was the first "new wave" show in Los Angeles. It wasn't punk yet—the word punk hadn't even been used at that time. A few hundred people showed up but it was mentioned in *Billboard* [magazine] and that really helped to establish the alternative, indie scene in Hollywood.[8]

Soon afterward, the Starwood and the Whisky started booking new bands.

In August 1976, radio station KROQ hired Rodney Bingenheimer, a former club owner and über music fan, as a disc jockey. From the beginning, Bingenheimer played the Ramones and Los Angeles bands the Dils and the Motels, making him one of the few people in the country playing punk on the radio. With the success of the Radio Free Hollywood concerts, KROQ began promoting shows, known as the KROQ Cabaret, featuring unsigned local bands.

By this time, news filtering over from England about British punk was influencing the developing Los Angeles scene. The Screamers, fronted by two performance artists from Seattle, Tommy Gear and Tomata du Plenty, were one of the first popular punk bands in L.A. "When the Screamers came to Los Angeles from Seattle, the punk thing was happening in England, and we decided in a conscientious way to have a sense of solidarity with it," said keyboardist Gear.[9]

Musician Peter Case also booked his own shows for his band, the Nerves. He rented out rooms, made flyers, and hired other bands to play. One of the first bands Case partnered with was the Weirdos, a group of art students who had formed in February 1977. After a few shows with the Nerves at the Orpheum Theater, the Weirdos quickly became L.A.'s top punk band. At the time, Weirdo Cliff Roman said, "In Los Angeles punk exists as against cultural stagnation. I think punk really means the extinction of hippie-dom. In each high school now there's a clique of kids into punk rock. They're cutting their hair short and probably getting beat up—and they aren't called punks, they're called weirdos."[10]

The Germs, with leader and singer Darby Crash, played their first show in the spring of 1977, opening for the Weirdos and the Zeros even though they had no songs and had only rehearsed a few times. In the coming year, the Germs would write manic snarling songs, incoherently sung, and release the first local punk single—"Forming"—on What? Records. Their first and only album, *GI*, was released in December 1979, one year before Crash committed suicide.

Then, in the summer of 1977, the budding Los Angeles scene got what it needed most: a regular place for punk bands to play. Mere months after Brendan Mullen opened a rehearsal space for bands in a basement just off Hollywood Boulevard, he was hosting all-ages shows featuring the bands that rented his rehearsal rooms. He christened the place the Masque. Word spread, and soon the Masque became the hub of a new scene, growing into a clubhouse for kids who were into art films, David Bowie, Iggy Pop, drugs, alcohol, and punk rock. As the crowds grew, other clubs noticed and began booking punk bands. Occasionally, groups like the Dead Boys or the Damned came through town, but L.A.'s punk scene was now powered by local bands.

> **HEAR IT HERE — INFLUENTIAL PUNK RECORD LABELS**
>
> **Alternative Tentacles:** Dead Kennedys, Butthole Surfers, D.O.A.
> **Dangerhouse:** the Weirdos, the Bags, the Dils, the Avengers
> **Dischord:** Minor Threat, Fugazi, Embrace, Jawbox
> **Epitaph:** L7, Bad Religion, NOFX, Rancid, the Offspring
> **Fat Wreck Chords:** NOFX, Propagandhi, Rise Against, Anti-Flag

As popular as Hollywood punk bands were, only one of them, the Dickies—something of a novelty act—were signed by a major label. In New York, many of the original CBGBs groups were signed by major record labels, but in other cities, including Los Angeles and San Francisco, the majors weren't interested. As a result, in Southern California, band members, friends, and fans of the bands started labels like What?, Dangerhouse, and Slash to get the music out.

The First Wave of American Punk: Cleveland

Cleveland, Ohio, had one of the earliest punk scenes outside of New York City. In 1974, the Mirrors, the Electric Eels, and Rocket from the Tombs (RFTT) were already playing a raw brand of music that would later be called punk rock. A short distance away, Akron, Ohio, had the Bizarros and Devo. It was a fertile scene, in part, because Cleveland radio exposed people to new bands that weren't commercially successful in the rest of the country. The New York Dolls and Television played there very early in their careers.

One of the most important Cleveland bands, now largely forgotten, was the Electric Eels. Calling their music 'art terrorism,' the band delighted in provocation and violence and, as early as 1974, wore what would later become emblematic punk clothing: safety pins and ripped shirts, T-shirts with insulting words scrawled on them, white power logos, and swastikas. They recorded one single, "Cyclotron," before breaking up in 1975.

The short-lived RFTT also broke up that year, spawning two well-known punk groups: Pere Ubu and the Dead Boys. With the iconoclastic and adventurous Pere Ubu, singer David Thomas released one of the first independent punk singles in the country, "30 Seconds over Tokyo," on the band's own Hearthan label. RFTT's guitarist and drummer, later known as Cheetah Chrome and Johnny Blitz, joined Frankenstein with singer Stiv Bators. After their 1976 audition at CBGBs, they became the Dead Boys and moved to New York where they were quickly signed by Sire Records. Like Pere Ubu, the Dead Boys used an old RFTT song for their first single. By 1977, most of the early Cleveland punk bands had broken up or moved to other cities.

Hardcore Punk

With the Hollywood punk scene in full swing in the late 1970s, twenty miles to the south a group of suburban kids, many still teenagers, were putting together their own bands. These bands used the short, fast songs of the Ramones and Britain's Sham 69 as a starting point but stripped the songs to the bone—no melodies, no solos, just a one or two minute blast of raw teenage anger. Between 1979 and 1986, this

Greg Ginn, second from right, with his hardcore band Black Flag at the 9:30 Club in March 1981. (© Bert Queiroz. Used by permission.)

new music, called hardcore punk or hardcore, became the sound of American punk. Led by Black Flag, the Dead Kennedys, and Bad Brains, hardcore spread across the country through an underground network of zines, mail-order records, and word of mouth. Hundreds of bands emerged, helping the scene grow and, in some cases, hastening its demise.

Guitarist Greg Ginn started Black Flag, first called Panic, in Hermosa Beach, California, in 1977. In time the band became influential not only for their hard sound but also by introducing a lot of cities to hardcore music through their frequent tours, by releasing music from other hardcore bands on their SST label, and for their unstoppable work ethic, which led to marathon rehearsals and endless tours. They were also the first to alter the sound and look of hardcore in 1983 by slowing down their songs and growing their hair shoulder-length.

By 1980 Black Flag had became synonymous with violence in Los Angeles, where their fans routinely battled police during and after shows. As a result, the band was banned from clubs and forced to play at parties, in rented halls, and anywhere else it could. At the same time, scores of new bands were popping up south of Los Angeles in the South Bay (Circle Jerks, the Minutemen), Fullerton (Social Distortion, Agent Orange, the Adolescents), and Huntington Beach (TSOL), where the most violent slam dancing originated. TSOL, in particular, was the epitome of a violent hardcore band. Described as high school jocks who got into punk, they wore leather jackets and leather engineer boots with chains and bandanas around them. Their singer, a tough guy named Jack Grisham, often wore makeup or a dress on stage, daring anyone to hassle him.

San Francisco's Dead Kennedys, led by singer Jello Biafra and guitarist East Bay Ray, may have done more than any other band to help break hardcore to audiences across the United States and Europe. According to writer Steven Blush, the Dead Kennedys "identified a nascent movement and nurtured it. They sought out like-minded artists, and aided many unknown upstarts. In their zeal to establish a united scene, DKs set the ground rules for everything Hardcore since Day One."[11] In 1978 the band was the first hardcore group to tour the East Coast—a miserable experience, but one that taught them how to run a tour. The following year they set out again, having released their first single, "California Über Alles." Biafra booked the shows, arranged to have local bands in each city open for them, and worked with promoters to make sure the bouncers didn't overreact and beat up enthusiastic fans. They introduced hardcore to Europe in 1980 after the release of their album, *Fresh Fruit for Rotting Vegetables*, and later used their own label, Alternative Tentacles, to release a compilation album called *Let Them Eat Jellybeans* with songs from other hardcore bands.

The most musically proficient hardcore band was Bad Brains, from Washington, D.C., who, at their peak in the early 1980s, were widely considered the best band in the hardcore universe. Formed in 1978 by a group of African American jazz-fusion musicians, Bad Brains played lightning-fast songs with astonishing precision while dynamic singer H.R. mesmerized the audience with his onstage gymnastics. They played so fast and so well, other bands feared having to open a show for them. "To us, Bad Brains meant everything," said Black Flag singer Henry Rollins, who grew up in Washington. "I have never seen anything like 1979–1980 Bad Brains, before or since. You thought they were going to detonate right before your eyes."[12]

After inspiring and mentoring Minor Threat and other Washington, D.C., bands, Bad Brains moved to New York City, helped the hardcore scene get off the ground there, and recorded their self-titled first album for the cassette-only label ROIR. When it was released in 1982, British music magazine *Sounds* called it "one of the true miracles to have emerged from punk rock."[13] Over time, as the band dove deeper into their Rastafarian lifestyle, they started playing reggae at their shows, disappointing many fans. Mercurial singer H.R., who quit the band several times, turned down record deals, and alienated people within the punk community, is largely blamed for the band's inability to establish a lasting musical legacy beyond hardcore.

> **HARDCORE IN THE HEARTLAND**
>
> Hardcore bands from the Midwest:
> **Chicago**—Naked Raygun, Big Black, the Effigies
> **Indianapolis**—Zero Boys
> **Milwaukee**—Die Freuzen
> **Detroit**—the Necros, Negative Approach, the Meatmen
> **Austin**—Millions of Dead Cops (MDC), Big Boys, Dicks
> **Houston**—Really Red, DRI

The hardcore era lasted until around 1986, by which time most of the original bands had broken up or changed direction. By its nature, hardcore was a very narrow musical form that appealed to young musicians. As the musicians grew more proficient, many wanted the opportunity to explore new styles.

Punk After Hardcore

Some in the punk scene thought the end of hardcore meant the death of punk as the punk scene splintered into a number of subgenres. Some groups, including TSOL, turned to a more hard rock sound that was very popular in the late 1980s. Others explored their passion for ska music (a style originating in Jamaica) and developed ska punk, and some began writing and performing music that was more melodic, innovative, and focused on expressing composers' emotional states beyond anger. This last genre, called emo, had such a lasting impact beyond the punk scene that by the late 1990s it was being used as a marketing tool to brand major-label bands.

Ska Punk

In the late 1970s, British bands the Specials, Madness, the Beat, and Selector created a distinctive fast, bouncy style of music by blending ska, reggae, punk, and pop. In 1987, Operation Ivy formed in the San Francisco area and played an energetic mix of ska with a heavier punk sound at the all-ages club the Gilman Street Project. They released an EP and an album on Lookout! Records and toured, influencing a number of young punks along the way. The band broke up in 1989, but a number of other ska punk bands came along later, finding a surprising level of mainstream success in the 1990s.

Emo

The term "emo" was originally used to describe a subgenre of punk that originated in Washington, D.C., in the mid-1980s as bands expanded the hardcore template with lyrics that were introspective and music that was less formulaic and more melodic. A number of bands on the Dischord Record label were key players in the early emo sound: Rites of Spring, Embrace, One Last Wish, Beefeater, Gray Matter, and Fire Party. Though most of these bands had broken up by the early 1990s, the emo moniker was later applied to commercial bands such as Fall Out Boy.

Pop Punk and Commercial Success

In 1991, a three-piece band from Seattle released a record that would change the look and sound of popular music around the world and bring punk rock back out into the spotlight. Nirvana's *Nevermind* went to #1 on the *Billboard* charts and sold, by some estimates, 26 million copies worldwide. This astonishing success led the major record labels into a feeding frenzy as they snapped up scores of punk bands along with the so-called grunge bands from Seattle. Green Day, a punk band that cut its teeth as teenagers playing at the Gilman Street Project, had a huge hit in 1994 with *Dookie*, their first major label release. Even bands that didn't sign to the majors found the public suddenly receptive to their music. Independent Epitaph records alone had three huge hits in 1994 with albums by Rancid, the Offspring, and NOFX. Soon a new breed of punk bands emerged, including Good Charlotte, Sum 41, and Blink-182, playing songs with hummable melodies and memorable choruses that led them to be labeled "pop punk." The term was rarely used with affection.

The magnitude of the success of these bands reignited a debate within the punk rock scene about what it means to be punk. Asked about bands such as Green Day, Ian MacKaye of independent Dischord Records responded, "I'm not critical of them at all. The only thing I will say is that they're not punk bands. There may be punks in the band, but there's no such thing as a punk band on a major label."[14]

As some had expected, these punk-inspired, if not exactly punk, bands have found long-term commercial success. "I'm surprised [success] took as long as it did with punk," says Jello Biafra. "Part of the reason I guess was the music was so intense it delayed the inevitable mass embrace. But I figured it was going to happen sooner or later. The music was too good."[15]

But pop punk bands are merely the contemporary commercial face of punk. Right now, across the United States another generation of young people are forming new bands, writing songs, and practicing in their basements and garages. There's no doubt that some of them will play punk, but we have no idea how they will sound.

> **HEAR IT HERE—MORE INFLUENTIAL PUNK RECORD LABELS**
>
> **Kill Rock Stars**: Bikini Kill, Bratmobile, Unwound, Sleater-Kinney
> **Posh Boy**: Social Distortion, Agent Orange, the Adolescents
> **Slash**: the Germs, X, Fear, the Misfits, Gun Club
> **SST**: Black Flag, Minutemen, Hüsker Dü, Sonic Youth, Meat Puppets
> **Touch & Go**: Butthole Surfers, Big Black, Jesus Lizard, Yeah Yeah Yeahs

Getting the Music Out: Independent Punk Record Labels

American music has had a long history of independent record labels run by enthusiasts who desired little more than to get the music they loved out to a wider audience and make a few dollars along the way. Labels such as Chess, Sun, Motown, and Blue Note were all at some point independent labels run by strong personalities: Leonard Chess, Sam Philips, Berry Gordy, and Alfred Lion. But by the mid-1970s, many independent labels had been swallowed by MCA, Polygram, RCA, Warner Brothers, and other corporate giants.

Sire, at the time an independent label run by Seymour Stein, was one of the few companies willing to take a chance on early New York punk bands. It signed the Ramones, Talking Heads, Dead Boys, and Richard Hell. Another independent, Private Stock, released Blondie's first album. The large labels, reluctant to invest money in artists who didn't meet prevailing tastes, relegated some of their new finds, Patti Smith (Arista Records), Television (Elektra), and the Dictators (Epic), to subsidiary labels. But because most bands had little chance of being signed to a major label, and there were few true independent labels in business, friends, fans, and band members began recording and releasing records on their own. In two early examples, Mer Records, which put out Patti Smith's first record ("Hey Joe"/"Piss Factory"), was financed by her friend, photographer Robert Mapplethorpe, and Television's manager, Terry Ork, released the band's "Little Johnny Jewel" single on his own Ork Records.

This trend exploded when hardcore punk arrived in the late 1970s. From Black Flag's Greg Ginn in Hermosa Beach, California, to Minor Threat's Ian MacKaye and Jeff Nelson in Washington, D.C., and the Dead Kennedys in San Francisco, bands took matters into their own hands and released their own music. Their subsequent labels—SST, Dischord, and Alternative Tentacles—were just three of the hundreds of independent record labels that arose between the late 1970s and early 1990s expressly to press music by punk or alternative bands.

NOTES

1. Interview with the author, October 2008.
2. *Punk* Magazine, www.punkmagazine.com.
3. Scrivani-tidd, Lisa M. *Greenwood Encyclopedia of Rock History, Volume 4* (Westport, CT: Greenwood Press, 2005).
4. Kristal, Hilly, "The History of CBGBs," installment 2, page 3, CBGB & OMFUG, www.cbgb.com/history/history9.htm.
5. Stark, James. *Punk '77* (San Francisco: RE/Search Publications, 2006), 68.
6. Vale, V., ed. *Search and Destroy #1—6, The Complete Reprint* (San Francisco: RE/Search Publications, 1996), 13.

7. Stark, *Punk '77*, 91.

8. Interview with the author, October 2008.

9. Mullen, Brendan, and Marc Spitz. *We Got the Neutron Bomb* (New York: Three Rivers Press, 2001), 65.

10. Vale, *Search and Destroy #1—6, The Complete Reprint*, 55.

11. Blush, Steven. *American Hardcore* (Los Angeles: Feral House, 2001), 103.

12. Anderson, Mark and Mark Jenkins. *Dance of Days* (New York: Soft Skull Press, 2001), 42.

13. Ibid., 104.

14. Interview with the author, May 15, 2009.

15. *Punk's Not Dead*, directed by Susan Dynner, 2007.

CHAPTER THREE

Gathering Places: Fanzines, Performance Spaces, Radio Stations, and Record Stores

The initial punk scene in New York began in one bar in one neighborhood where many people already knew each other. As punk spread across the country, influenced primarily by news about British punk bands and a few of their early British punk records, small groups of like-minded people in various cities started to put on punk shows, stock punk music in their record stores, write and distribute fanzines about punk, and play punk on the radio. Within a few years, an infrastructure was established that connected punks with each other and allowed a diverse subculture to develop. The key places where punks could meet others, hear music, or learn more about the punk were performance spaces, fanzines, radio stations, and record stores. This essay looks at just a few of each of these in an attempt to show how widespread, yet diverse, punk subculture became in the United States.

Performance Spaces

Clubs

From one end of the country to the other, small clubs gave punk fans a chance to hear and talk to new bands and meet other punk fans. These small clubs also gave local bands an opportunity to perform—and, in some cases practice—their original songs and develop their own style. For just a few dollars a night, people could socialize, drink, and dance to music they might not have found on the radio or in record stores. By the early 1980s, most major American cities had a club that specialized in punk, new wave, or underground music—the club that was known as the place to go to hear what was happening outside of mainstream music.

Several punk clubs became ground zero for the local music scenes that eventually developed in their cities. Here are a few of the clubs that gave punk fans many fond memories and, in some cases, helped kickstart the entire local music scene:

CBGBs—New York City—From 1973 to 2006, Hilly Kristal ran CBGBs, the most famous punk rock club in the United States, and one of the longest-running, in lower Manhattan. Considered the birthplace of U.S. punk in the 1970s, the club also became home to hardcore bands in the 1980s. For years the club featured hardcore punk matinee shows on Sunday afternoons, helping launch the careers of the Cro-Mags, Agnostic Front, Sick of It All, and other bands. After a long-standing dispute over the club's lease and unpaid

Famed New York punk club CBGBs in November 1993. (AP Photo/Jim Cooper)

rent, in 2006 Kristal put on a series of high-profile farewell shows. At 1:00 a.m., on October 16, Patti Smith sang her ballad "Elegie" and read a list of punk musicians and advocates who had died since the club opened. It would be the last song ever performed at CBGBs.

Mabuhay Gardens—San Francisco—The Mabuhay Gardens, a former Filipino nightclub, was the anchor of the San Francisco punk scene from 1977 to the early 1980s, giving local bands a regular place to perform and grow and their audience a place to meet and hang out. Just a few months after Jeff Olener of the Nuns convinced the "Mab's" owner, Ness Aquino, to let his band play there, the Mab converted to a full-time rock and roll club, and a local scene was born. Says Olener,

> There was no media coverage at all. We made it totally unique and no one knew about it. It was a well-kept secret, except for a few hip people. And for the first six months of 1977 it was fabulous because it was like your own private scene you had created. . . . It was artists, writers, photographers, filmmakers, musicians all different cool people mixed up.[1]

In the coming years, the club booked some of the best early punk bands, including the Ramones, the Damned, the Dead Kennedys, and D.O.A. After 1982, Aquino opened his doors to heavy metal bands before closing in 1986. Several attempts to reopen the Mab, most recently in fall 2007, have failed.

9:30 Club—Washington, D.C.—Founded by Dody DiSanto and Jon Bowers, the 9:30 Club, named after its original address at 930 F Street, NW, was Washington's home for alternative and punk bands in the early 1980s. When the club began allowing fans as young as sixteen to enter, it became the center for hardcore punk, often showcasing local bands such as Bad Brains, Minor Threat, Government Issue, and Scream. Legendary musicians from Richard Hell to Black Flag, the Minutemen, Social Distortion, and Nirvana all played the small club, with its 200-person capacity. In 1996, the club moved into a remodeled music hall, enlarging its capacity to 1,200. Still a stalwart location for live music in Washington, the 9:30 Club continues to book an eclectic mix of just about anything under the sun.

The Masque—Los Angeles—In the summer of 1977, Scotsman Brendan Mullen rented the basement of the old Cecile B. DeMille building on Hollywood Blvd where he could live, practice drumming, and rent cheap rehearsal space to bands. As bands started throwing all-night parties, Mullen began hosting free shows with any musicians willing to play in the basement, now called the Masque, without professional lights, a stage, or an adequate sound system. In February 1978, *Los Angeles Times* writer Kristine McKenna described her visit to the club:

> As one descends into the club, the air grows dank and stale. Lighting consists of an occasional naked red or blue bulb. Ceiling tiles have been ripped away leaving a polka dot network of dried glue splotches. Graffiti, the predominant décor, is everywhere. Layers of it in day glow colors adorn every inch of the club. . . . Winding hallways running from the central concert area lead to rehearsal rooms where stained carpet scraps have been tacked up for acoustic insulation. Some flea-bitten mattresses and abandoned refrigerators give the place the look of a hippie crash pad.[2]

From this less-than-humble beginning, the Los Angeles punk scene exploded. To Mullen, the Masque was a cooperative venture where bands and staff were paid little but punks and musicians could hang out almost any time. The Masque had no liquor license, so all ages were admitted and the bands could play all night long. "After the Pistols hit and the Damned, then the first wave of bands, the Weirdos, Germs, Skulls, the Bags, and the Eyes and the whole Masque scene started,"[3] said Loren Molinare, guitarist for the Dogs. "You talk about fashion and counterculture—you didn't have to be pretty, you didn't have to be anything, just who you were, and I think that was the whole magnet to that Masque scene—the disjointed, outcast generation. It was very primitive: 'Let's start a band. We can't play.'" In its first year, the police and the fire marshal shut the club several times, leading Mullen to hold a Save the Masque Benefit in February 1978. The proceeds saved the club for a time, but by 1979 Mullen was forced to close the Masque for good.

La Mere Vipere—Chicago—Started by Noah Boudreau, Rick Faust, John Molini, and Mike Rivers as the city's first punk disco in May 1977, La Mere Vipere held its first "Anarchy Night" on Mother's Day. In June, after staging "Punk-O-Rama," a three-day event featuring films, live performances by local bands, and a fashion show, they transitioned the club from a part-time gay bar/punk club to a full-time punk bar. There, at the height of the disco music craze, people danced to records by the Ramones, the Sex Pistols, and the Dead Boys and their inspirational ancestors, Iggy Pop and David Bowie. When a suspicious fire destroyed the club on April 27, 1978, the scene shifted to Oz (1977–1981) and O'Banions (1978–1982). Naked Raygun, Black Flag, Hüsker Dü, D.O.A., Minor Threat, the Dead Kennedys, and TSOL all performed for Chicago punk fans at one or both of these clubs.

688 Club—Atlanta—From May 1980 to November 1986, the 688 Club, a converted biker bar, was Atlanta's home for punk, new wave, and alternative music. Founders Steve May, Sheila Browning, and Tony Evans opened the club to put on shows by new national acts and the local bands coming out of Athens, Georgia, including REM, Pylon, and Love Tractor. The list of bands that played the 688 Club reads like a who's who of early 1980s hardcore and punk, but the audience was just as likely to hear "new wave" bands or American roots rock. With the drinking age only eighteen at the time, the club's young audience hung out regularly and fans of all sorts started to blend together. According to David T. Lindsay, a regular 688 patron, "What punks always said about destroying the barriers between the audience and the band, 688 actually did. You had a rapport with the bands and stuff. You were right next to them, and you could talk to them."[4]

The Rat—Boston—The Rathskeller, called "The Rat" by locals, was open from 1974 to 1997 in a basement under a bar/restaurant in Boston's Kenmore Square area. The Boston punk scene was just getting under way in 1975, when the Rat started booking local bands Willie "Loco" Alexander, the Real Kids, and DMZ. In the next few years, the club also brought in most of the groups from the CBGBs scene and British visitors such as the Police and Elvis Costello. In time, the Dead

Kennedys, Mission of Burma, Agnostic Front, Bad Brains, Sick of It All, and Boston-area hardcore bands SSD, Toxic Narcotic, and the F.U.s played the club. The Rat was closed in 1997 and razed in 2000. In the mid-1980s, much of the hardcore punk scene moved to the Channel nightclub, which had opened in 1980 and also booked reggae and classic rock shows.

The Bird—Seattle—The first punk club in the city, the Bird was opened in downtown Seattle in 1978 by Roger Husbands. Though its official capacity was ninety-nine, on any given night many more packed into the dark, narrow, warehouse-like space with a makeshift stage and a secondhand PA system. Local punk bands the Mentors, Red Dress, and the Enemy played the Bird, as did the Dils and the Zeroes, from California. After fire marshals closed the first Bird (a common fate of many punk clubs), a second version was opened on Capitol Hill, at the spot that later became the Century Ballroom.

Bookies Club 870—Detroit—In 1978 Don Was (later of Was/NotWas) and a partner booked a punk show at Frank Gagen's, a former Detroit supper club known as Bookies. In March, after Detroit's first punk band, the Sillies, played Bookies, the band took the club over, making it into the only punk club in the city. Bookies soon became the first stopping point in the Midwest for many bands from New York and Great Britain and was home to local bands the Romantics, Sonic Rendezvous, and Destroy All Monsters. Over time, other punk clubs sprung up, drawing away some of Bookies' audience. Eventually the Sillies severed their ties with the club. The building burned down in the late 1980s.

Collectives and Nonprofit Performance Spaces

In many cities, the punk scene included a large number of teenagers under drinking age. For them, the all-ages shows in collectively run, nonprofit performance spaces such as the 924 Gilman Street Project in Berkeley, ABC No Rio in New York City, and the Mr. Roboto Project outside Pittsburgh provided entry to the scene. These ventures, which showcased the true do-it-yourself (DIY) spirit of punk by relying on volunteers, remain open and committed to all-ages shows and upholding a code that prohibits racist, misogynistic, and homophobic bands or material.

924 Gilman Street Project—Berkeley, California—This all-ages, nonprofit, collectively organized music and performance venue was founded in 1986 by Tim Yohannan and others from the fanzine *Maximum Rocknroll*. Tired of the neo-Nazi/skinhead audiences they found in punk clubs in the mid-1980s, as well as policies that forced bands to pay clubs to play and the brusque bag searches required before club entry, the founders wanted to create a space for punk music that was run by and for the punks. Since December 31, 1986, the Gilman Street Project has put on several punk or hardcore shows each weekend and offered art exhibits, speakers, and other events for young people. The Gilman Street Project relies on its members/volunteers to staff each event and weigh in on how things are run. If a patron or band member doesn't like the way the club operates, they are given a simple message—get involved and change it. Members of several popular punk bands, including Green Day and Rancid, spent their teenage years playing at 924 Gilman Street.

ABC No Rio—New York City—A month after CBGBs ended their hardcore matinees in November 1989, ABC No Rio, a collectively run center for art and activism on the Lower East Side, opened their doors to the punk bands who were willing to play in a room without a stage or stage lighting. Later the basement was converted into a club-type space with a sound system, basic lighting, and a small stage. Records and T-shirts were sold upstairs, and literature from animal rights groups, Greenpeace, and other similar organizations was handed out. ABC No Rio had been founded in an abandoned tenement at 156 Rivington Street in 1980 by a group of artists committed to political and social engagement and oppositional culture. The artists in the collective use the living room–like first floor for art shows, spoken-word performances, and live music. As of 2009, ABC No Rio's matinee hardcore/punk shows continue. Their policy states, "We are committed to creating a diverse and inclusive scene where all can feel welcome and comfortable, regardless of race, gender or sexual identity. We do not book racist, sexist or homophobic bands."[5]

The all-ages Mr. Roboto Project outside Pittsburgh, Pennsylvania, in June 2009. (© Sharon M. Hannon.)

The Mr. Roboto Project—Wilkinsburg, Pennsylvania—In the late 1990s, with few options in the Pittsburgh area for punk, hardcore, and independent/alternative shows, a small group formed a cooperative to create a comfortable and open space for people to experience a true DIY community. They located an empty storefront in Wilkinsburg, just outside the Pittsburgh city limit, and put on their first show on November 12, 1999. Along with punk and hardcore shows, Roboto features performance art, art shows, and other types of performances. To keep things running, Roboto relies on the energy and ideas of its volunteers and members. Members, who pay minimal yearly dues, book the shows at Roboto, meet monthly, help keep the space clean, and enforce the rules. Modeled after the Gilman Street Project, Roboto reserves the right to refuse to work with any performer or promoter based on the message or content of the material to be performed (i.e., no racist, sexist, or homophobic material).

Alternative Performance Spaces

As punk bands proliferated from Massachusetts to Minneapolis, from Akron to Austin, many played anywhere they could. In addition to music clubs, punk scenes relied on alternative performance spaces— VFW halls, basements, youth centers, high school gyms, empty warehouses, abandoned churches—to give bands the opportunity to play and to reach young audiences who could not yet get into nightclubs. Bad Brains, Minor Threat, and other bands in Washington, D.C., for example, put on all-ages shows in high schools and in the basement of the Wilson Center, which housed an employment center and free clinic. By the late 1980s, alternative performance spaces became essential to the punk scene as few clubs continued to book punk bands. Most underground music scenes, by their very nature, were born in alternative performance spaces, and these unusual venues continue to offer young people the opportunity to experiment and develop their local punk scenes.

Fanzines

Almost as soon as punk began, young writers, artists, and photographers in New York City—and then across the country—began chronicling their local punk scenes in homemade fanzines or zines. By 1977, punk zines were popping up everywhere, giving the world such publications as *New Order* (Dania, Florida), *Fanzine for the Blank Generation* (Tustin, California), *Cawabanga* (Midland, Michigan),

Record Raves (Stone Harbor, New Jersey), *Teen Titans* (Overland Park, Kansas), *Gulcher* (Bloomington, Indiana), *Twisted, Stab Your Back,* and the *Gabba Gabba Gazette* (all from Chicago, Illinois), *It's Only a Movie* (Fairfax, Virginia), *Frenzy* and *Licks* (Boston, Massachusetts), *Chatterbox* (Seattle, Washington), *Vintage Violence* (Silver Spring, Maryland), *Generation X* (North Hollywood, California), *Can't Buy a Thrill* (Baton Rouge, Louisiana), *Future* (Rochester, New York), and hundreds of others. Most zines were typed and then reproduced on copy machines. Their pages weren't numbered. Until national distribution systems were established in the 1980s, most zines were sold for a dollar or less at punk shows or in bookstores, record stores, and any place else that would take them. Some lasted only a few issues, while others lived on for several decades and were the first to print the work of writers, photographers, and artists who went on to wider mainstream success. In this way, these fanzines made a lasting contribution to popular culture beyond punk while also providing the glue that brought the punk scenes together.

Below are just a few of the thousands of punk zines that have existed since three guys from Connecticut created the magazine that gave punk rock its name.

Punk—In 1975 three high school friends—John Holmstrom, Ged Dunn, and Eddie (Legs) McNeil—and fans of the New York band the Dictators, started a magazine. As McNeil tells it, "Holmstrom wanted the magazine to be a combination of everything we were into—television reruns, drinking beer, getting laid, cheeseburgers, comics, grade-B movies, and this weird rock and roll that nobody but us seemed to like: the Velvets (Underground), the Stooges, the New York Dolls, and now the Dictators."[6] McNeil suggested they call it *Punk*. After interviewing Lou Reed and the Ramones for their first issue, they papered New York with WATCH OUT! PUNK IS COMING posters. With Dunn as publisher, Holmstrom as editor and illustrator, and McNeil as "resident punk," they released their first issue on January 1, 1976. Hand-lettered and illustrated by Holmstrom, *Punk* was part *Mad* magazine, part comic book, and part *Creem* magazine. It was the first publication that focused on the bands playing CBGBs, but its irreverence, humor, and inanity, reflecting the sensibilities of its creators, were a big influence on fanzines to come. After fifteen issues,

Punk folded in 1979. Holmstrom later put out a couple of special issues and tried to restart the magazine in 2001, and again in 2007.

Search and Destroy—In 1977, V. Vale, an employee at San Francisco's City Lights bookstore, created a magazine to chronicle the punk scene happening at Mabuhay Gardens. With $100 from Allen Ginsberg and matching funds from his boss Lawrence Ferlinghetti, Vale published the first issue of *Search and Destroy*. He frequently referenced the Dada and Surrealist movements and ran interviews with some of his favorite writers—J. G. Ballard and William Burroughs—and artists in other media alongside articles about punk bands and punk heroes Iggy Pop and Lou Reed. *Search and Destroy* listed information for fan clubs, bands, and fanzines in other cities and had a glossary of punk terms and personalities. Vale, who encouraged his graphic designers to experiment with the text, photos, and layout, later started RE/Search Publications "to explore the irrational shadow of official culture."[7] In 1996, RE/Search Publications released two volumes containing reprints of all eleven issues of *Search and Destroy*.

Slash—Steve Samioff and Claude Bessy founded this influential Los Angeles fanzine in 1977. Bessy, a native of France, was the fanzine's primary writer, editor, and record reviewer. His vitriolic rants against mediocrity, the music industry, and the mainstream were published under his punk nom de plume, Kickboy Face. In the first issue, he wrote:

> So there will be no objective reviewing in these pages, and definitely no unnecessary dwelling upon the bastards who've been boring the living s*** out of us for years with their concept albums, their cosmic discoveries and their pseudo-philosophical inanities. Enough is enough, partner! About time we squeezed the pus out and sent the filthy rich old farts of rock 'n' roll to retirement homes in Florida where they belong.[8]

Bessy soon became a spokesperson for L.A. punk. In its almost four-year lifespan, *Slash* was the first magazine to seriously cover the Hollywood punk scene along with the bands coming out of England and New York, and it helped the L.A. scene coalesce. "If it wasn't for

Slash and the other zines, or Kristine McKenna writing for the *L.A. Times*, the scene would never have become what it became," said John Doe, bassist for X. "Gradually it created a local music scene because it was being publicized."[9] Over time *Slash*'s agenda expanded—stories about the Weirdos, the Dils, and the Germs were accompanied by interviews with filmmakers and writers. By 1979 Samioff had partnered with Bob Biggs, who founded Slash Records, released albums by X and the Germs, and shut down the magazine within the next eighteen months.

Flipside—One of the longest running punk zines, *Flipside* was first published in Los Angeles in August 1977 by founder and editor Al Kowalewski and a group of other former students from Whittier High School. Beginning its life as a photocopied and stapled quarter-page zine devoted to the early L.A. punk bands, *Flipside* evolved into a full-color, glossy magazine. *Flipside* released three vinyl fanzines in the 1980s with hardcore punk bands and a compilation album in 1993. Flipside Records also released albums by Babyland, M.I.A., Detox, Bulimia Banquet, and Doggy Style and finally shut down in 2000.

Maximum Rocknroll—This San Francisco Bay area fanzine began its life as a spinoff of the popular Maximum Rocknroll rock radio show. The zine first appeared in 1982 as the newsprint booklet included in "Not So Quiet on the Western Front," a compilation album released on the Dead Kennedys' Alternative Tentacles label. Editor Tim Yohannan, in his early 40s, encouraged a left-wing, politically activist bent in punk, so much so that he was often attacked verbally for brow-beating and name-calling those who didn't share his philosophies. He became an extremely controversial figure in punk rock, but he also deserves credit for connecting punk scenes through the international scene reports published in *Maximum Rocknroll*. Now, over twenty-five years and 300 issues later, *Maximum Rocknroll* and its all-volunteer staff continue to produce an independent, not-for-profit publication that features punk bands of all stripes alongside articles detailing punk scenes and political and activist news from around the world.

Covers from three early fanzines: Punk, Maximum Rocknroll, *and* Jet Lag. *(Collage designed by Stephanie Helline. © Jet Lag. Used by permission.)*

Profane Existence—This magazine was established in 1989 in Minneapolis, Minnesota, to cover the international activist and anarcho-punk movement. Relying on a volunteer staff and outside writers, photographers, and artists, the magazine created a worldwide network of contributors, subscribers, and distributors that submitted interviews with bands, artists, activists, and publishers, as well as opinion columns, letters from the community, news and current events, and music, print, and video reviews. Since its first issue, *Profane Existence* has also focused on issues relevant to people in prisons and has been made available to them at little or no cost. As a product of the DIY punk community, the staff publish a wide range of articles (e.g., self-help guides, vegan recipes) and work closely with hundreds of DIY bands, labels, publishers, distributors, and other organizations. In 1992 *Profane Existence* and *Maximum Rocknroll* co-published *Book Your Own F***in' Life*, a directory of bands, distributors, venues, and houses where touring bands or traveling punks could sleep, and sometimes eat, for free. Until 2008, Profane Existence Records released a number of albums from political punk bands and crust punk bands such as Doom, Misery, Fleas and Lice, Anarcrust, Counterblast, Dirt, and Hellbastard. To give readers more regular updates and defray growing printing costs, in early 2009, *Profane Existence* began publishing a Web magazine available by subscription. They also set up Coopdistro.com, a marketplace and auction site for DIY punk, metal, and hardcore items.

Punk Planet—In 1994, Daniel Sinker established this influential and well-respected zine in Chicago. *Punk Planet* focused on the broader punk subculture in articles about politics, visual arts, feminism, and other progressive issues and became renowned for its in-depth, thoughtful interviews with artists and activists. *Punk Planet* released several books with collections of these interviews. After thirteen years and eighty issues, problems with their distributor and mounting financial pressures forced *Punk Planet* to cease publication in 2007. As the editors wrote in their farewell letter,

> We've also done everything in our power to create a support network for independent media, experiment with revenue streams, and correct the distribution issues that have increasingly plagued independent magazines. . . . Benefit shows are no longer enough to make up for bad distribution deals, disappearing advertisers, and a decreasing audience of subscribers.[10]

Punk Planet Books remains in business, and its Web site continues to function as a place where "independently minded folk" can network.

Forced Exposure—From the early 1980s to 1993, *Forced Exposure* was published in Massachusetts by Jimmy Johnson and Byron Coley. Known for long interviews, caustic, sarcastic reviews, and stories tinged with a bit of humor, the zine covered punk and independent music but also contained stories about counterculture figures who included William Burroughs, Charles Bukowski, and Nick Zedd. Musicians Steve Albini and Lydia Lunch were among its contributors. *Forced Exposure* continues to distribute CDs and vinyl records.

Radio Stations

Many of the pioneering punk rock radio shows were broadcast on college radio stations with only a few watts of power, but even that was enough to attract new fans. Even in Midwestern cities not known for their punk scenes, one show on a small station could make a difference. Steve Pick, a student living in St. Louis in the late 1970s, recalls, "There was a college radio station at Washington University, KWUR, which was 10 watts and you could barely pick it up ten miles away. But every Friday and Saturday night there were these shows that played all these new records and that was my religious ritual every week to listen to that and hear what was going on." Pick later cofounded *Jet Lag* fanzine, which brought punk news to St. Louis for more than a decade.

WZRD—Chicago—On Northeastern Illinois University's student radio station, DJ Terry Nelson's "Sunday Morning Nightmare" show featured some of the first punk heard on Chicago airwaves. The show was highly influential in the early 1980s; Chicago area musician and record producer Steve Albini called it the "one radio program" for Chicago punk rock in the 1980s. WZRD still offers Chicago an alternative to other stations by providing what they call creative, freeform programming.

WMBR—Boston—In the late 1970s, the Massachusetts Institute of Technology's radio station (at that time under the call letters WTBS) was only 10 watts, but it broadcast one of the first punk radio shows in the United States, hosted by a DJ known as Oedipus. In 1977, DJ Tom Lane increased the station's commitment to punk by broadcasting a show called the "Late Risers Club," from 10:00 a.m. to 1:00 p.m. every Monday to Friday, although at first the DJs had to pad the show with reggae and some hard rock to make up for the lack of punk records. The "Late Risers Club," now a weekly radio show, continues to bring punk rock to the greater Boston airwaves.

WGTB—Washington, D.C.—The radio station for the conservative Jesuit-run Georgetown University may seem like an unlikely station to have first championed early punk, but WGTB had a history of coming under fire for the liberal/radical politics espoused on some of its programming. If the political content grew too heated, from time to time the university would shut the station down. In March 1976, the entire staff was fired and the station went off the air for three months. When it returned, DJs Steve Lorber, John Paige, Myron Berthold, and others with an open ear for the new helped launch the D.C. punk scene by playing bands from CBGBs, Pere Ubu, and new local acts Overkill and the Slickee Boys.

KPFA—San Francisco—In 1977, Tim Yohannan and Jeff Bale started the "Maximum Rocknroll" radio show to get punk music on the airwaves. Later joined by Ruth Schwartz, Jello Biafra, and others, Yohannan and Bale mixed leftist politics with band interviews and created one of the first radio shows that focused on hardcore music from around the globe. The show became so successful it was eventually broadcast from stations across the United States and abroad and can still be heard on a number of U.S. stations as well as online. The radio show was the precursor to the *Maximum Rocknroll* zine, which began in 1982.

KROQ—Los Angeles—Rodney Bingenheimer's show, "Rodney on the ROQ," which began in 1976 and continues to this day, has been arguably the most important punk rock radio show over the past three decades. Bingenheimer has introduced scores of new American and British punk bands to his audience, which included most members of the early Southern California punk and hardcore scenes. Members of the Germs and Black Flag personally handed Bingenheimer their first recordings, which he played religiously when few in radio were even aware of the coming hardcore movement.

Record Stores

Record stores have been extremely important to the punk subculture. A local record store represented not only a place to buy music, but also a place to hang out, chat with the owners and employees, meet other punk fans, listen to new music, and get educated about what was really going on in the local music scene. Many cities were lucky to have even one store that stocked punk music. Below are a few stores where punks unearthed the music that changed their lives.

Yesterday and Today—Rockville, Maryland—Former DJ Skipp Groff opened Yesterday and Today just north of Washington, D.C., in September 1977. Groff planned to cater to music buyers looking for obscure 1960s records, but when his punk record sales overtook all others, the store expanded its stock of punk music. Called "Y and T" by locals, the store was just what the D.C. punk scene needed. While punks shopped, they could listen to tapes of local bands that Groff played in the store. When Groff eventually started his own label, Limp Records, his first release was the *Mersey Mersey Me* EP by the Slickee Boys, at the time the top punk band in the area. After twenty-five years, Groff closed the brick-and-mortar store in 2002, but he continues to sell 45s, LPs, and CDs online.

Bleecker Bob's Golden Oldies—New York City—Originally called Village Oldies, Bleecker Bob's opened in Greenwich Village in 1967 at the height of the hippie era. But when the New York punk scene exploded, owner "Bleecker Bob" Plotnik, never one to shy away from trends, enthusiastically stocked the latest punk records, both British and American, along with posters and the occasional bootleg record. Other New York stores also carried punk records, but Bleecker Bob's was known for having the best selection. One of New York City's oldest independent record stores—they still carry more vinyl than CDs—Bob's continues to attract all types of music fans.

Rather Ripped Records—Berkeley, California—For a time in the mid-1970s, Rather Ripped Records was the place for underground and noncommercial music, including punk, in the San Francisco Bay area. The store specialized in imports, collectibles, and independent and import material not generally available in the United States. On her first trip to California in 1974, Patti Smith read her poetry in the store, and in 1979, the Police made an in-store appearance. The owners also ran a mail-order business called the Dedicated Fool.

Extreme Noise Records—Minneapolis, Minnesota—This punk record cooperative opened in Minneapolis on April 1, 1994, to serve the punk scene of the Upper Midwest, which didn't have a record store dedicated to punk music. The store carries the latest releases from punk bands around the world as well as classics from the 1970s and 1980s, music from local bands, and plenty of 12- and 7-inch vinyl. With an all-volunteer staff, Extreme Noise Records reinvests any profits back into the shop and other punk music projects. In its Best of the Twin Cities, 2008 edition, Minneapolis' *Citypages* voted Extreme Noise Records the best place to buy punk and heavy metal—though it's doubtful there was any real competition.

Many communities still have a brick-and-mortar store that specializes in, or at least features, punk music. Some of these stores have been in business for years and have weathered the changes in the marketplace as music moved from vinyl to CD to digital downloads. In Seattle, Singles Going Steady is known for great punk music, and in Princeton, New Jersey, the Princeton Record Exchange buys and sells hardcore punk CDs and records. Open since 1980, the Exchange calls itself one of the largest independent punk record stores on the East Coast, with over 140,000 titles.

Surprisingly, as many big record chains have closed in recent years, some smaller, specialized stores have opened. In Orange County, California, for example, the punk record label TKO opened a store in October 2007. TKO specializes in collectible punk on vinyl, but it also makes room for other musical genres and sells punk T-shirts and clothing.

NOTES

1. Stark, James. *Punk '77* (San Francisco: RE/Search Publications, 2006), 13.
2. McKenna, Kristine. "Punk Is Underground—Literally," *Los Angeles Times*, February 10, 1978, G24.
3. Interview with the author, October 2009.
4. Clark, Jeff. "688 Club," *Stomp and Stammer*, October 2008, www.stompand stammer.com/index.php?option=com_content&id=1542&Itemid=51&task=vie w&limit=1&limitstart=2.
5. ABC No Rio, "Saturday HardCore/Punk Matinee," www.abcnorio.org/events/ punk.html.

6. McNeil, Legs, and Gillian McCain. *Please Kill Me* (New York: Penguin Books, 1996), 203.
7. Hodgkins, Leslie. "RE/Search History," *Researchpubs.com*, www.researchpubs.com/Blog/?page_id=151.
8. Bessy, Claude. "So This Is War, eh?," *Slash*, volume 1, issue 1, May Day Issue, 1977.
9. Mullen, Brendan, and Marc Spitz. *We Got the Neutron Bomb* (New York: Three Rivers Press, 2001), 83.
10. Sinker, Daniel. "Punk Planet Magazine—R.I.P.P.," *Punk Planet*, June 18, 2007, www.punkplanet.com/pp_blog/punk_planet_magazine_r_i_p_p.

Punk Fashion
and Art

Punk Fashion

From 1975 to 2009, numerous punk fashions and hairstyles have come into vogue, each driven by punks' desire not to conform, to look different or threatening, and to simultaneously say "we are not like you" to mainstream culture and "we belong" to other punks. Yet, over time, each fashion incarnation has been appropriated by mainstream culture. A trip to any suburban shopping mall can turn up people with messy hair, dark eyeliner, T-shirts with politically or socially confrontational messages, tattoos, piercings, leather jackets with the names of bands stenciled on the back, work boots, or Chuck Taylor All-Stars shoes— all styles popularized by punk culture. As a result, new punk styles continue to arise as punks attempt to remain outside the norm.

Early punk styles were developed in opposition not only to the disco craze that was sweeping the nation in the late 1970s, but also to the hippies of the mid-1970s with their long hair, brightly colored clothing, bell-bottom pants, and sandals. Punk fashion New York style, as exemplified by musician/writer Richard Hell, was a rejection of all things hippie: black straight-leg pants, black leather jackets, short spiky hair, and torn T-shirts held together with safety pins. Hell scrawled his own words across his clothes ("Please Kill Me" on one shirt).

The Sex Pistols' manager Malcolm McLaren readily admits he copied Hell's style and took it back to England, where he and Vivienne Westwood ran a boutique. There they combined Hell's homemade deconstructionist clothing with bondage and leather gear, renamed the boutique *Sex*, gave some clothes to the Sex Pistols, and started selling the rest to punks with money. Their torn shirts emblazoned with words

Punk fashions on display at the Fun Fun Fun Fest in Austin, Texas, November 9, 2008. (© Lisa A. Hernandez. Used by permission.)

such as "Anarchy" and "Destroy," deliberately provocative shirts and jackets featuring Nazi swastikas and safety pins, and Doc Martens (English work boots), leather jackets, and bondage gear became the first internationally recognizable punk style—and the one still most associated with punk.

Despite the DIY ethos in punk, almost from the beginning punk clothing was commercialized and marketed to punks. Sure, bands like the Clash who couldn't afford to buy clothes in punk stores still spray-painted or stenciled their clothing while others, like the Ramones, basically wore what they had at home. But some bands and, more important, some of their audience, shopped for style.

By July 1977, New York City had its first punk store, Manic Panic, run by sisters Tish and Snooky. There, punks or people who wanted to look punk could buy wild hair dyes, T-shirts, spike-heeled stiletto shoes, go-go boots, fishnet stockings, vintage clothing from the 1950s, leather jackets, tight black pants, and theatrical cosmetics. The store still remains open, having weathered many changes in the mood and culture of the country.

Also in 1977, a Los Angeles fanzine, *Punk Rock*, featured an article entitled "How to Look Punk."[1] It offered these suggestions:

- Cut up T-shirt, then lace or pin it back together.
- Hand-paint words on T-shirts (graffiti) then decorate with pins, 1-inch size buttons, etc.
- Jeans with pins.
- Make vest out of black plastic trash bag, wear over long sleeve T-shirt. Decorate with graffiti.
- Self-mutilation and body piercings.
- Loads of hair, or no hair.

There were regional variations in punk attire. Unlike the leather jackets and dark clothing favored by New York bands, the clothing Los Angeles punks crafted from thrift store and Salvation Army discards often included bright, shocking, well-worn or tattered gowns, coats, and jackets. Ripped stockings, sheer fabrics, underwear worn on the outside, and garbage bags were added to the bondage pants/safety pin styles seen on the British punks. The Hollywood punks seemed to want to dress up and be noticed, break a few taboos, and have fun.

In much of the country, Americans interested in punk were still influenced by post-hippie fashions. It took a number of years for flared pants and long hair on men to disappear, replaced by straight leg pants and irregular hairdos, along with neon shades of pink, blue, and green hair made possible by Crazy Color hair dye.

By the early 1980s, the hardcore scene ushered in a period of antifashion: men now sported shaved heads or crew cuts, T-shirts,

Punks show off their hairstyles at the Fun Fun Fun Fest in Austin, Texas, November 9, 2008. (© Lisa A. Hernandez. Used by permission.)

jeans, motorcycle boots or Doc Martens, and studded belts. For a time it was popular for girls in the hardcore scene to wear plaid skirts. Soon, tattoos, once worn soley by biker groups, men in the military, and drifters, became popular. The British punk scene popularized the use of safety pins as adornment, particularly through the cheek, though few punks actually sported this ornamentation. The safety pin later gave way to exotic piercings, adopted from the underground world of S&M and brought into the light by punks beginning in the 1990s.

The most extreme and easily recognized punk hairstyle, called the Mohawk or Mohican, came into fashion in the early 1980s. This hairstyle could be twisted to form large spikes along the top of the head, known as Liberty spikes. Even today, the hairstyle remains one of the clearest indicators that punks are present.

With punk in its third decade and segmented into many sub-subcultures, punks wear clothing to identify with their specific group. Some incorporate elements from 1970s British punk or the 1980s hardcore scene. Others wear camouflage pants, jackets with patches and messages, and studded vests. The popular skate punk style includes baggy shorts or jeans, hooded sweatshirts (called hoodies), and skate shoes made by Vans and other popular brands.

In 1989, a store called Hot Topic opened its doors in Westminster, California, and within a few years had established a reputation for selling music-inspired fashion to masses of teenagers. If bands—be they punk, metal, or hard rock—were wearing it, Hot Topic sold it. Cross necklaces, bracelets, band T-shirts, hair dyes, body jewelry, and all types of punk clothing and accessories were made available in malls in all fifty states—no DIY required.

Hundreds, perhaps thousands, of online stores such as Starlets and Harlots and Too Fast Clothing now offer punk clothing, shoes, bags, and punk accessories: necklaces, belts, rings, and ankle cuffs. Dogpile punk rock clothing claims to offer original independent punk rock clothing and declares war against the mass-produced punk clothing sold in malls and produced in China. "Don't be a fool, buy yer Punk Clothes from real punks, not from corporate scumbags looking to cash in on yer rebellion," their Web site warns.[2] Even in the world of online commerce, the competition is on to appear more punk than the other guys.

Punk Art

Just as there is no universally agreed-upon definition of punk, the qualities that constitute punk art also vary, although there are a few generally agreed-upon characteristics. Punk art, the artwork created for punk album covers, flyers, and posters or made by punks to decorate their own clothing, fanzines, or Web sites, has often been designed to shock, outrage, or disturb mainstream culture. It may also incorporate elements of political and social commentary, although it may be absurdist, humorous, angry, or serious.

Many early punk artists repurposed images and text using a cut-and-paste or collage style to create their commentary and jolt viewers out of complacency. The infamous Sex Pistols' logo and graphics were made up of letters of different sizes and fonts designed to look as if they were cut from a newspaper. Resembling a ransom note, the Pistols' logo immediately suggested something illicit, a bit dangerous, and definitely outside the norm.

"Collage is an expression of angst—it's quick, fast, and easy," says artist Winston Smith. "It graphically came out looking chaotic and disorganized. It was like, 'Listen to me!'—which was also what the music was all about. It's not any easier than painting or sculpture, but was a quick way for people to render an image without having to learn to draw like Raphael."[3] Smith had a long association with the San Francisco punk band the Dead Kennedys, beginning in 1981 when the band used his piece, *Idol*, on the cover of their EP *In God We Trust, Inc.* In this piece, Smith commented on religious hypocrisy by showing the figure of Jesus Christ, shiny and gold like a bowling trophy, crucified on a cross made of dollar bills with a bar code above his head reading 666.

Another artist, Mark Vallen, says, "I've always been interested in oppositional culture and the shock of the new, so when the punk rock movement hit Los Angeles in the Seventies, I immediately recognized it as fertile ground for expressions of dissent and cultural insurrection and wasted no time in joining the ranks of the blank generation."[4] While studying at the Otis Parsons Art Institute of Los Angeles, Vallen was influenced by African American social realist Charles White. Vallen's work incorporates social and figurative realism, whether he is drawing punks, members of Southern California's Latin American community, or other ethnic groups struggling with civil rights issues in the United States. Beginning in the late 1970s, Vallen created a number of drawings, prints, and paintings of his experiences in the Los Angeles punk scene. His 1980 cover for the last issue of the fanzine *Slash* was entitled "Come Back to Haunt You," and featured a leather-clad Native American with a Mohawk, which may have presaged the Mohawk haircut craze among Los Angeles punks. To Vallen, the image suggested that the spirits of Native American warriors had come back to possess the youthful punk rebels of the United States. He saw the punk phenomenon as "an opportunity to challenge the established order by helping to create an energetically contentious culture. Punk turned accepted aesthetics and notions of 'normalcy' upside down, it admonished the complacent and demanded that people be more than a witness."[5]

British artist Gee Vaucher is best known for her work in the late 1970s and early 1980s with the anarcho-punk band Crass. As the creator of some of the most disturbing and acclaimed images of the time, Vaucher expressed her pacifist and feminist views through collages and paintings. Working at first in black and white because the band could not afford to reproduce color artwork for their album covers, Vaucher's in-your-face art mirrored the band's political sensibilities and expressed the need for social change. According to Mark Vallen, "Vaucher's early works for Crass were intellectually sophisticated, technically well crafted, and dare I say—beautiful. Full of narrative and profound meaning, they wielded a social critique as pertinent today as when they first appeared decades ago." For her 1980 piece entitled *"Who do they think they are fooling?—You?"* Vaucher took a famous photo of the Sex Pistols and replaced the band with the Queen of England, Pope John Paul II, the Statue of Liberty, and Margaret Thatcher all decked out in various punk attire: leather pants, jackets, jeans, and a T-shirt with the word "Destroy" scrawled across it. As Vallen says, "If the Pistols were a rock 'n' roll swindle, Vaucher was telling us, then the icons in her artwork represented the ultimate ruling class con job."[6]

Vallen, Smith, and a number of other artists who began their careers by creating punk art have now found their works collected and housed in prestigious art galleries. Artist Raymond Pettibone's early work is most often associated with the Los Angeles hardcore scene and the band Black Flag. He designed Black Flag's distinctive four-bar logo along with flyers, posters, and album covers for other bands on the

Flyers advertising shows by Teen Idles, the Replacements, and Black Flag illustrate the different style and quality of the artwork bands used in the 1980s. (Angelos Archive; collage designed by Stephanie Helline.)

SST record label. His work, characterized by black-and-white illustrations, some with provocative captions or text, is now in the permanent collections of the Museum of Modern Art in New York, the Museum of Contemporary Art in Los Angeles, the San Francisco Museum of Modern Art, and others.

In 1992, artist Aaron Rose and four friends founded the Alleged Gallery in New York City. Over the next decade, Alleged Gallery evolved into a fertile ground for art world outsiders as Rose curated shows featuring work by skateboarding and graffiti artists. When works by these artists began to appear in mainstream art galleries, Rose curated the exhibition "Beautiful Losers: Contemporary Art & Street Culture," a large-scale traveling exhibition celebrating the spirit behind this artistic movement. He codirected a film of the same name that looked at the newly successful artists and, in perfect punk fashion, questioned whether a person can become successful and still maintain the original motivation for their art. As the film's promotional materials ask, "What happens when the outside becomes 'in'?"[7]

The lighter and more humorous side of punk art can be seen in the work of illustrator John Holmstrom, one of the founders of *Punk* magazine. Inspired and taught by cartoonists Will Eisner and Harvey Kurtzman, the originator of *Mad* magazine, Holmstrom's brightly colored cartoons with hand-lettering stand in stark contrast to some of the darker images associated with punk. "Roy Lichtenstein and Andy Warhol were the biggest fine art influences on the punk thing, but one cultural influence that's been forgotten is 1970s minimalism," he said. "There was a concerted effort by bands like Suicide, the Ramones and Talking Heads to follow the aesthetic that 'less is more' and to strip music down to its core. Blow it up and start all over again!"[8] As for the lasting impact of punk on art, Holmstrom says:

> I think today's lowbrow art movement, as seen in *Juxtapoz* maga-
> zine, has been influenced by punk in a big way. The East Village art
> scene was also punk-inspired. One common element to these move-
> ments as well as *Punk* magazine is an appropriation and appreciation
> of popular culture—usually the more shocking and bizarre images.
> Also common is an approach to illustration that's representational,
> but not necessarily realistic. It's not careful, it's casual. We're not try-
> ing to capture reality; we're trying to create a new one. There's also
> an element of humor, which is usually alien to "art."

In true DIY spirit, punks around the world have created their own artwork for their fanzines and Web sites. In the precomputer years, this work required creative use of scissors, glue, and the Xerox machine to design collages and rough, yet striking, images. With the advent of inexpensive graphics software, even the least artistically inclined punks can use a computer to express themselves and their unique design sense.

NOTES

1. The Go-Gos Notebook, "1977 Punk Fashion Couture," http://gogonotes.blogspot.com/2008/03/1977-so-what-are-you-gonna-wear.html.
2. Dogpile Clothing, www.dp-77.com/home.php.
3. Blush, Steven. *American Hardcore* (Los Angeles: Feral House, 2001), 290.
4. Mark Vallen's Art for Change, "Punk Portraits," www.art-for-a-change.com/Punk/punk.htm.
5. Kantor Gallery, "Critical Visions," www.kantorgallery.com/press/2003/critical-visions-2003-artofpunk.htm.
6. Vallen, Mark, "Peace, Love, and Crass Art," Mark Vallen's Art for Change, www.art-for-a-change.com/blog/2008/01/peace-love-and-crass-art.html.
7. Beautiful Losers, www.beautifullosers.com/film.html.
8. Heller, Stephen. "Putting the Punk in DIY: An Interview with John Holmstrom," AIGA, www.aiga.org/content.cfm/putting-the-punk-in-diy-an-interview-with-john-holmstrom.

| # Women in Punk

There were a lot of women in the beginning. It was women doing things. Then it became this whole macho anti-women thing. Then women didn't go to see punk bands anymore because they were afraid of getting killed. I didn't even go because it was so violent and so macho that it was repulsive. Women just got squeezed out.[1]

—Jennifer Miro, singer for the Avengers

Punk opened the door for female musicians and singers who were just as removed and disaffected from mainstream culture and the status quo as their male counterparts and who had been told for years that they could not play their instruments well or properly. The early days of punk were a high-water mark for women musicians as female drummers, bassists, and guitarists joined bands around the country with or without the much-accepted female lead singer. Punk's disinterest in virtuosity, as well as its lyrical content and focus on style, gave women more access to the subculture's core than they had experienced in any previous American youth subculture.

In *Pretty in Punk*, Lauraine Leblanc's study on women in punk, the author notes that "early punk was the first rock scene in which women and sex were not the main focus of song lyrics, allowing punk music to avoid gender stereotyping in large measure."[2] Although the Dead Boys and the Stranglers were noted for their misogyny, overall the early days of punk were an empowering time for women.

But this first phase of punk did not last long. As the 1980s dawned, punk music morphed into hardcore, a brand of aggressive hyper-masculine music commandeered by a new contingent of faster, more aggressive bands. As hardcore, with its hard-hitting slam dancing and thrash, spread from Southern California, it often took over from the diverse and artier punk scenes that had formed after 1976. Women soon found themselves increasingly on the outside looking in, or not looking at all.

From 1976 to 1980, women musicians, photographers, and other artists seemed to be everywhere in punk, working to help their local scenes develop. The musicians were the most visible. In Los Angeles, the protopunk all-female band the Runaways put out their first album in 1976. Though much disparaged as a tool of their promoter/manager, the group recorded and toured with various lineups until 1979. The band produced two guitarists who had successful careers in the 1980s—Joan Jett and Lita Ford—and greatly influenced Darby Crash of the Germs. Crash later tapped Jett to produce the Germs' one and only LP, *GI.*

Mary Kay, bassist for the Dogs, and Martha Davis, singer for the Motels, were part of the group behind Los Angeles' first rock and roll DIY project, Radio Free Hollywood, in which bands who couldn't get booked into regular rock clubs started putting on their own shows. The bands rented a hall, bought beer, hired a security guard, and made flyers to advertise. The success of these shows made the established music promoters take notice and ultimately kicked the door open for new bands to get played on the radio and booked into clubs.

YES, SHE CAN PLAY!

Some Female Guitarists:
Donita Sparks and Suzi Gardner (L7), Brody Dalle (The Distillers), Poison Ivy (The Cramps), Lulu Gargiulo (The Fastbacks), Erin Smith (Bratmobile), Corin Tucker and Carrie Brownstein (Sleater-Kinney), Joan Jett

In New York, bands in the original punk scene were replete with women. Although still outnumbered greatly by men, the community that sprung up around CBGBs brought the world Patti Smith, Debbie Harry (Blondie), Tina Weymouth (Talking Heads), Poison Ivy (The Cramps), and Annie Golden (The Shirts).

One of the more outrageous punk bands of the time, Sic F***s, was fronted by sisters Tish and Snooky Bellomo. With a reputation for their shocking and irreverent style, the sisters created their own elaborate outfits that included ripped nuns' habits with rosaries, bottles of holy water, shredded black silk stockings, and garter belts. In July 1977, they took their sense of style to the marketplace and opened Manic Panic on St. Marks Place. Having a real punk store in the city helped ratify punk style for the public. There, punks too lazy or otherwise unwilling to create their own fashions could buy T-shirts, hair dye, leather jackets, and other punk-related accessories.

On the West Coast, women punks were also highly visible. Two of the most popular early San Francisco punk bands, the Nuns and the Avengers, featured lead singers Jennifer Miro and Penelope Houston. In Los Angeles, Exene Cervenka sang for X, Alice Bag fronted her band, the Bags, and Lorna Doom played bass for the Germs.

By the late 1970s, a second wave of bands arose in New York City, ushering in even more outspoken and arresting women such as Lydia Lunch of Teenage Jesus and the Jerks. The Jerks, with singer, writer, poet, and spoken-word artist Lydia Lunch, were members of the short-lived "no wave" movement, a group of bands who played abrasive, cacophonous noise/music as a rejection of and response to what they saw as the commercialization of punk and its reverence of past rock and roll and R&B. Though Lunch had admired Patti Smith and Television, she said she "wanted to create something that would completely divorce myself from that, break away and shoot forward. I still found that a lot of things that I was drawn to didn't go far enough or were still too based in a tradition."[3] The Jerks spurned CBGBs and other traditional music clubs and performed in alternative spaces in New York City. The influential Brian Eno–produced *No New York* LP, released in 1978 and featuring the Jerks and other no-wavers, inspired Sonic Youth and other future punk offspring.

As punk scenes in major U.S. cities slowly developed, women contributed to the scenes through their work as photographers, writers, managers, artists, clothing designers, and record producers—an area almost off-limits to most women even today. "Punk was great for women. Punk helped women a lot," recalls photographer Erica Echenberg. "You know if you were a woman you could be in a group, a drummer or a singer. You could do anything you wanted. You could be a fan. You could be a photographer and nobody cared really. . . ."[4]

When the Dead Boys' manager and CBGB owner Hilly Kristal needed a producer to take his band into the studio for the first time, he hired Genya Ravan, who became one of the first female producers to be hired by a major record label. Although she seemed an unusual choice to produce this undisciplined, debauched band of misfits, Ravan's work with the Dead Boys on their debut *Young, Loud, and Snotty* captured the band in all of their raunchy rock and roll glory. Ravan also produced demos for New York bands the Shirts and the Miamis.

Many of the early punk photographers were women: Roberta Bayley, Stephanie Chernikowski, Ebet Roberts, and Eileen Polk are just a few of the women who captured the downtown New York music scene and the first wave of British punks in the late 1970s. Before buying a camera in 1975 and becoming chief photographer for *Punk* magazine, Bayley worked at CBGBs, which allowed her to meet many of the punk pioneers. One of the first photographers to shoot these new bands, Bayley shot the iconic cover photo of the Ramones' first album and the covers for Richard Hell and Johnny Thunders records. She went on to capture many classic early punk images before hanging up her camera in the 1980s.

Another famous album cover, *The Clash*, was taken by photographer Kate Simon, an American living in England when punk exploded. Simon later returned to the U.S. and took photos of Debbie Harry, Patti Smith and counterculture idols William Burroughs and Andy Warhol.

Photographer Cynthia Connolly got her first taste of punk in her native Los Angeles. "In 1980 in L.A. it felt like there was this huge community of all different kinds of kids—some were into drugs, some were into the music. I was into the punk scene because it felt like I could contribute something and it didn't matter if

---

YES, SHE CAN PLAY!

Some Female Bassists:
Kim Gordon (Sonic Youth), Kim Deal (Pixies), Melissa Auf der Maur (Hole, Smashing Pumpkins), Jennifer Finch (L7), Kira Roessler (Black Flag), Lorna Doom (The Germs), Kim Warnick (The Fastbacks), Kathi Wilcox (Bikini Kill), Mary Kay (The Dogs)

I was a girl or a boy. There was some kind of movement and it had to do with art and music."[5]

When she moved to Washington, D.C., in 1981, Connolly found the punk scene was made up of guys who were into hardcore music from England and bands like the U.K. Subs and Stiff Little Fingers. "It was mostly guys but everyone was nice," she says. "I wanted to be involved in some kind of music or art scene that was open-minded and [where] women were treated equally as men. [The D.C. punk scene] was a small community and I just latched onto it. I thought it was cool that these kids were 14 and 15 and putting out records and recording. It was like one big family." But over time, as the scene became more masculine, Connolly started to lose interest and moved to San Francisco to work for *Maximum Rocknroll*. She later returned to Washington and compiled *Banned in DC*, a book of photos and anecdotes from the Washington, D.C., punk underground from 1979 to 1985.

Many women also worked for fanzines as writers and graphic designers. Filmmaker and writer Mary Harron began her career with *Punk* magazine, writing an article about the Ramones for the very first issue. Harron went on to write for a wide-range of publications including the *Village Voice*, *Melody Maker*, and *New Musical Express*. She later cowrote and directed the films *Who Shot Andy Warhol*, *American Psycho*, and *The Notorious Betty Page*.

But the depth and strength of women's involvement in punk changed as the hardcore movement spread across the country and the scene became more masculine and violent. At punk shows, the audience that once jumped up and down or pogoed now slam-danced and thrashed against one another in the mosh pit, or "the pit," the area in front of the stage. Girls who took their chances in the pit were subjected to the same pushing and shoving as the guys, as well as some groping. "The hardcore scene that followed in the wake of early U.S. punk virtually killed the female element and diversity of the early scene," says Danny Furious, former drummer for the Avengers. "Women were afraid to attend gigs because you literally took your life in your hands if you tried to enter the mosh pit."[6] In the 1983 film *Another State of Mind*, a punk named Baca remarks, "You can get hurt, you can, if you're a girl. From a girl's point of view I don't think that slamming's advisable . . . I think it's pretty stupid. It's a good way to get your aggressions out if you're a guy." Roxie, another punk, explains, "I used to slam dance. I used to be the only girl out there slam dancing. And I got my leg broken."[7]

As the hardcore scene grew, fewer and fewer women were active as band or audience members. In Washington, D.C., where women had played in Urban Verbs, the Slickee Boys, the Nurses, Tru Fax and the Insaniacs, Tiny Desk Unit, the Shirkers, and other early punk bands, women found themselves on the outside by as early as 1981. In the late 1970s, women made up half the audience at shows, but their attendance dwindled as the shows and the slam dancing in the pit became more ferocious and dangerous. According to Nathan Strejeck of the Teen Idles, "When TSOL and Circle Jerks came out with vinyl, slam dancing got big . . . all the girls who went to the shows sort of dropped out of the scene because it became so male-dominated. They kind of stayed on the outskirts."[8] Only a few women, including Kira Roessler, who played bass for Black Flag and appeared on five of their albums, played in hardcore bands.

Whereas early punk initially seemed to offer women opportunities for expression, hardcore stopped their progress in its tracks. Filmmaker Peter Stuart, who documented the hardcore punk scene with his partner Adam Small in *Another State of Mind*, came to the conclusion in 1983 "that women were just as repressed in punk cultures as everywhere else . . ."[9]

Wendy O. Williams (or WOW) was one exception. From 1977 to 1988, Williams, with her band the Plasmatics, channeled her aggression and rebellion into literally explosive shows highlighted by destruction, thrash, and caterwauling vocals. A self-confessed exhibitionist, Williams appeared onstage clad in underwear or bondage gear, often wearing little more than whipped cream or black electrical tape over her nipples. She was the first woman to appear on American television with a Mohawk. For one video, she famously drove a school bus through a pile of televisions and later skydived nude for a *Playboy* photo shoot—the only way she would agree to be in the magazine.

Williams and her partner Rod Swenson assembled the Plasmatics in 1977. Built as a concept band of revolving musicians around Williams with Swenson as manager, they released *Meet the Plasmatics* on their own Vice Squad label the following year. But the band's music was soon secondary to their live shows, which increasingly turned into full-frontal assaults on the senses as Williams cut televisions in half with a chain saw or smashed them with a sledgehammer while the

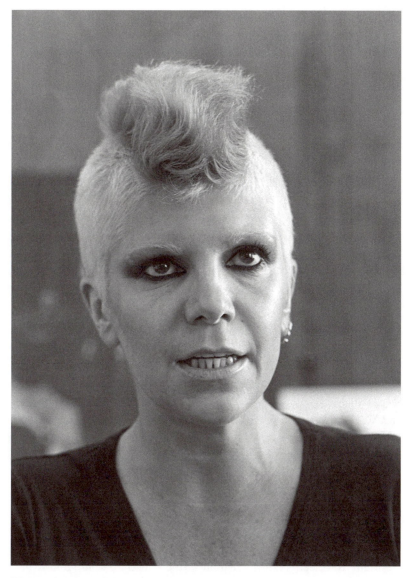

Plasmatics' singer Wendy O. Williams in Cleveland, Ohio, on April 8, 1981, for her obscenity trial. She was acquitted of the charges. (AP Photo)

band churned out heavy metal riffs at lightning-fast speed. In 1979, Williams blew up a car onstage at New York City's Palladium and later repeated the act on Tom Snyder's *Tomorrow* show. "With the Plasmatics," she said, "I have the opportunity to do what I love, which is smash these things and show they are just things. People in our society, I think, place too much value on material things." Williams saw these acts as a rejection of capitalism with its focus on material possessions, while others viewed them as publicity stunts. By 1983 the band had signed with Capitol Records and moved more toward a heavy metal sound, foreshadowing the blending of heavy metal and punk that would become commonplace by the end of the decade. Williams released eight studio albums before retiring from music in 1988.

By then, a strong musical underground had grown around the country, spread from city to city by independent records and the zines being produced in Austin, Minneapolis, Seattle, Boston, and elsewhere. Although they were greatly outnumbered by all-male groups, a number of groups included women: Sonic Youth (Kim Gordon), Pixies (Kim Deal), Beat Happening (Heather Lewis), and old stalwarts the Cramps (Poison Ivy). Punk's basic DIY message of personal empowerment and independence from authority continued to appeal to women, and as the first wave of hardcore bands broke up, a new generation of young women emerged, having grown up feeling marginalized in the very subculture that attracted them. Though they found little room in the punk scene, which

---

YES, SHE CAN PLAY!

Some Female Drummers:
Maureen Tucker (Velvet Underground), Dee Plakas (L7), Tobi Vail (Bikini Kill), Molly Neuman (Bratmobile), Janet Weiss (Sleater-Kinney)

---

had grown sexist and violent, they continued to play instruments, form bands, write songs, and create zines.

By the early 1990s, a number of women-focused punk zines such as *Bitch*, *Girl Germs*, and *Jigsaw* were giving women a forum to express themselves. To challenge sexism in punk, Olympia, Washington, resident Kathleen Hanna created a zine called *Revolution Girl Style Now* with her friend Tobi Vail and another, *Bikini Kill*, with Kathi Wilcox. The three women then formed a band, Bikini Kill, and moved to Washington, D.C., with the all-female band Bratmobile for the summer of 1991. During that summer, members of both bands, along with other women from the D.C. punk scene, began a new zine, *Riot Grrrl*, and put out a call for girls to come to a meeting to talk about punk rock and feminism. They began meeting weekly to discuss skills sharing—creating fanzines, playing instruments, putting on shows—with the goals of creating a new society that empowered women and introducing a new generation of women to feminism.

The movement that grew out of that summer, Riot Grrrl, encouraged young women to produce and create their own art and music rather than passively consume mainstream culture or the punk subculture that they had helped to shape. And they committed to helping other grrrls. For example, the bands began calling on the crowds to create a grrrls-only space where they could dance without getting hurt. Bikini Kill even released a statement outlining the Riot Grrrl philosophy.

That same summer in Olympia, independent record label K Records opened its International Pop Underground (IPU) Convention with "Love Rock Revolution Girl Style Now," a show devoted to female bands: Bratmobile, Bikini Kill, Heavens to Betsy, L7, Mecca Normal, 7 Year Bitch, and the Spinanes. The concert showcased the merger of punk rock and feminism and was credited with encouraging other Riot Grrrl bands to become more confrontational about gender politics.

By 1994, Riot Grrrl chapters had sprung up around the United States, Canada, and England, and the movement had caught the attention of the mainstream media. As stories about Riot Grrrl appeared in *Newsweek*, *Rolling Stone*, and *Entertainment Weekly*, the women who started the movement began to feel they were being misrepresented in the press. At first they launched a media ban, but when they saw their aesthetics and ideas being co-opted for marketing purposes, they distanced themselves from the movement. Says Kathleen Hanna,

> It's scary to see something that at one point in time was really important to you turned into a sound bite. It's gross when things like Riot Grrrl or feminism become a product. It's like, "Let's get it into as many magazines as possible so then everyone will know about it." I don't necessarily think that's the way to go about things because that's still reproducing a market economy. That's still saying, "Here are the managers that know the product that's best for you and you're just the stupid consumers that are supposed to consume it."[10]

Brody Dalle, singer/guitarist for the Distillers, performs on July 18, 2003, at the Lollapalooza festival in Clarkston, Michigan. (AP Photo/Paul Warner)

In the new century, the debate about gender roles in punk continues, as it does in American culture at large. Although women remain active in many aspects of punk/alternative culture, they are still remarkably underrepresented in punk music. In 1993, only one female band, Babes in Toyland, played on the Lollapalooza tour of alternative bands.

At the 2009 Vans Warped Tour in San Francisco, seven of the thirty-four bands, or 20 percent, featured women. The headliners were all-male bands. So, perhaps there has been some progress—if slight. That talented women such as Brody Dalle (The Distillers and Spinnerette) and Karen O (Yeah Yeah Yeahs) are credited for exuding strength *and* sex appeal on their own terms, when similar claims were made about Chrissie Hynde (The Pretenders) in the late 1970s, begs the question: how much has really changed?

As author LeBlanc has written: "Despite the critique of a breakaway faction (Riot Grrrl), at the beginning of its third decade of resistance, revolt, and refusal, punk remains a predominantly white, masculine youth subculture. Punk is still a site where girls remain marginalized and silenced."[11]

NOTES

1. Stark, James. *Punk '77* (San Francisco: RE/Search Publications, 2006), 93.
2. LeBlanc, Lauraine. *Pretty in Punk* (New Brunswick, New Jersey: Rutgers University Press, 2002), 44.
3. Perfect Sound Forever. "Lydia Lunch Interview." www.furious.com/perfect/ lydialunch.html.
4. A History of Punk Rock in 1977, "Erica Echenberg, Part 2." www.punk77.co .uk/punkhistory/ericaechenberg2.htm.
5. Interview with the author, January 17, 2009.
6. Academic Computer Club Umea University, "Danny Furious of the Avengers Interviewed." www.acc.umu.se/~samhain/summerofhate/avengersinterview.html.
7. *Another State of Mind*, DVD, directed by Peter Stuart and Adam Small, 1984.
8. Connolly, Cynthia, Leslie Clague, Sharon Cheslow. *Banned in DC* (Washington, D.C.: Sun Dog Propaganda, 1988), 25.
9. *Los Angeles Times*, October 28, 1983, G19.
10. Sinker, Daniel, ed. *We Owe You Nothing* (New York: Akashic Books, 2001), 65.
11. LeBlanc, *Pretty in Punk*, 64.

CHAPTER SIX | # Punk in the Media: Newspapers, Television, and Movies

Mainstream American newspapers, magazines, and television networks have had a contentious relationship with punk. The media's limited interest in punk has generally focused on the subculture's unconventional fashions or the violence and drug use that has plagued the scene at times. This was particularly true in the 1980s, the decade that brought the country the Dead Kennedys' obscenity trial, rampant reports about violence in the hardcore scene, the Parents' Music Resource Center (PMRC)—who successfully lobbied Congress to hold hearings about sex and violence in music—and Parents of Punkers and Southern California's Back in Control Training Centers, organizations created to help parents deal with punk children.

Yet even as they were being portrayed as deviants, punks ramped up production of their own media—radio shows, fanzines, and later Web sites and videos—where they could talk about music and cultural and social issues. If the mainstream media wouldn't talk about the positive aspects of the punk scene, punks would at least talk about them with each other.

Newspapers and Magazines

The 1970s New York punk scene flew under the mainstream media's radar for most of its brief heyday. What press the bands other than Patti Smith, an early favorite of rock critics, received before 1976 consisted of a few mentions by writer John Rockwell in the *New York Times*. During this period, the term "punk" was used arbitrarily as writers struggled to define it. In one early example in 1975, the *Washington Post* featured the article "Putting the Punk in Rock'n'Roll," a story about Bruce Springsteen—a man few people would classify as punk. When the Ramones first toured the country in 1976, some critics described them as the latest punk rockers in a long line that began in the 1950s with Elvis Presley and Gene Vincent. Lamenting the band's lack of musical ability, *Los Angeles Times'* critic Robert Hilburn labeled the Ramones "the final extension of the punk-rock movement."[1] To some, it seems, the movement was over before it really began.

For most Americans though, punk appeared in 1977 when the U.S. media latched on to the more visually stunning look and antisocial behavior of British punks. When the Sex Pistols muttered obscenities during a British television interview in December 1976, it caused a massive outcry. Great Britain's *Daily Mirror's* headline screamed "The Filth and the Fury!" Picking up on the outrage, the *Los Angeles Times* ran three stories about the band in the next five days. Other news organizations also reported the controversy, and before long American journalists were off to England to find out about the odd looking, ill-mannered British punks. In their stories, every punk had a safety pin through his/her cheek and wore a leather jacket and combat boots. The more provocative aspects of punk attire (i.e., Nazi swastikas and German World War II medals and uniforms) received far more attention than the more common hand-lettered T-shirts and spray-painted pants and jackets.

In June 1977 *New York Times* columnist William Safire wrote about the punk phenomenon in an article entitled "Punk's Horror Show." Calling punk the "new nihilism" and "one extended, mocking snicker," he summarized by saying "the brief and meteoric emergence of punk is rooted in a satiric reminder of the potential for brutality that lurks in every one of us."[2] Although Safire and other journalists focused almost exclusively on the British punk scene, the mainstream media would seldom have anything favorable to say about American punk for years to come. As a result, the music industry began promoting the term "new wave" in an effort to make punk palatable to a larger audience.

The Sex Pistols' arrival on American shores in January 1978 sparked a media circus manipulated by their manager Malcolm McLaren to create controversy and get as much free press as possible. It worked. Reporters followed them on their seven-show tour of mostly southern states, filing stories about the band's crude behavior, loud music, and unusual appearance. An NBC News Report for the *Today Show* called them "outrageous, vile, and profane" and their music "loud, totally unmelodic, primal, driving, and as ugly as the young men make themselves." By February 1979, when Sex Pistol Sid Vicious died of a heroin overdose, he had become the poster boy for punk's decadence and nihilism.

When the hardcore scene started in Southern California, the media's glare grew even more intense. By 1981, the *Los Angeles Times* was running regular stories on violence in punk, with Black Flag getting the most press—and subsequently getting banned from many Los Angeles clubs. Yes, there were favorable reviews of Circle Jerks and TSOL shows and Black Flag albums from critics Craig Lee and Jeff Spurrier, but much of the coverage was concentrated on the violence at the shows and the punks' battles against the police.

News organizations also frequently covered groups like Parents of Punkers and Back in Control Training Centers, who worked with parents to wean their children off punk and heavy metal. In "Taking control of a punk who happens to be your kid," a March 1986 *Chicago Tribune* story on Back in Control, the paper outlined the group's methods, which encouraged parents to remove all punk and heavy metal materials from the house, demand the child get an appropriate haircut, and throw out punk/metal clothing.

Television

Punk-related stories in televised news reports generally focused on violence at concerts, drug use, and vandalism while ignoring any aspect of punk's entrepreneurial DIY spirit. In some cases, the punks

PUNKS ON THE TUBE: FIVE GREAT PUNK MOMENTS ON TELEVISION

A Midsummer Night's Rock (NBC TV, 1970)

Iggy and the Stooges: On this broadcast of the June 13, 1970, Cincinnati Pop Festival, the Stooges perform "TV Eye" and "1970" while singer Iggy Pop, wearing a dog collar and ripped jeans, crowd surfs and spreads peanut butter on his chest. In their only television appearance, the Stooges prove that their stage show, and Iggy's fashion sense, were indeed ahead of their time.

Saturday Night Live (April 17, 1976)

Patti Smith: The queen of the New York punk scene performs "Gloria," with its infamous opening line: "Jesus died for somebody's sins but not mine." Smith would be the only punk on the show until the Clash in 1982, though by then the band had hit the big time and its members were no longer the snarling malcontents of 1977.

The Tomorrow Show with Tom Snyder (May 20, 1981)

The Plasmatics: In their second appearance on Snyder's show, the band races through "Head Banger" and "Master Plan" while lead singer Wendy O. Williams blows up a car on stage.

lived up to their press. During a 1981 performance by the Los Angeles punk band Fear on *Saturday Night Live*, punks from Washington, D.C., and New York City tore up the television studio. Newspapers the next day reported that the punks had done thousands of dollars worth of damage. Hardcore bands would never again perform on *Saturday Night Live* or any other network television show.

Many of the most fervent antipunk news reports and television shows came from Southern California, the center of the early hardcore scene. In 1982, KABC-TV in Los Angeles ran a news special: *We Destroy the Family: Punks vs. Parents*, featuring Serena Dank, founder of Parents of Punkers. Dank also appeared on *Donahue*, the *Today Show*, *Hour Magazine*, and other nationwide television programs to talk about her group sessions designed to get parents and punks to communicate.

That same year, two network television shows had punk-themed episodes that influenced not only parents who had children into punk rock, but also young kids attracted to the energy and violence of punk as represented on these shows. An episode of *Quincy, M.E.*, starring Jack Klugman, told the story of a troubled teenage girl interested in hardcore punk who gets mixed up with a murder that takes place at a punk club. The episode featured a band, Mayhem, slam dancing, and violence. Quincy visits a punk club and describes the experience: "The music I heard said that life was cheap and that murder and suicide was okay." In a January 1982 episode of *CHiPs*, punks steal guitars, slam dance, destroy vehicles, and cause a riot. The detective show *Simon and Simon* and *After School Special* also broadcast stories about drugged hardcore kids.

The media often made the mistake of equating the skinhead culture with the punk culture, primarily because they liked some of the same bands and favored close-cropped haircuts. By the mid-1980s, many skinheads, known for their extreme patriotism and propensity for violence and drinking, supported white power movements. Some punks also liked to fight and drink, but their politics more often veered to the left. Punks were more likely to burn a flag than attack an immigrant. On a 1986 episode of the *Phil Donahue Show* ostensibly devoted to the New York hardcore punk scene, which had become home to skinheads and straight edge fanatics, the host read some overtly racist lyrics by the skinhead band Agnostic Front without any mention of difference between the two subcultures. Donahue later attempted to broaden the discussion by allowing a few punks in the audience, as well as musicians in the Cro-Mags and Agnostic Front, to talk about the diverse nature of the bands and their fans and their DIY approach to life.

Saturday Night Live (October 31, 1981)

Fear: While this Los Angeles punk band performs "Beef Bologna" and "New York's Alright if You Like Saxophones," a group of Washington, D.C., and New York City punks in the studio slam dance, stage dive, and fight. As Fear starts into "Let's Start a War," the producers cut to a commercial, depriving the viewing audience of watching punks celebrate Halloween by throwing pumpkins around and trashing the studio.

48th Annual Grammy Awards (February 8, 2006)

Green Day: The little band from Northern California performs "American Idiot" amid lasers, strobe lights, and jets of fire. They later win Record of the Year for "Boulevard of Broken Dreams." Punk strides out into the mainstream. Or is it even still punk?

Green Day's Billie Joe Armstrong performs at the 47th Annual Grammy Awards on February 13, 2005, in Los Angeles. (AP Photo/Kevork Djansezian)

Music Television

For several years after MTV began broadcasting in 1981, the network refused to show punk videos even though the Minutemen and a few other bands were already making inexpensive videos. Suicidal Tendencies' "Institutionalized" was finally picked up in 1983 and played routinely amid Michael Jackson songs, but this was an anomaly. Not until 1991, when Nirvana had their huge hit "Smells Like Teen Spirit," did grunge/punk videos find a place in the regular rotation. Even then, the videos played were produced by bands on major labels who were selling a lot of records. Most bands on small, independent labels didn't seem to exist for MTV.

In the 1990s, as punk music became big business, a new generation of bands, including Green Day, Offspring, and Rancid found television more receptive, introducing punk to a larger audience and leading to its broader commercialization. After the shoe company Nike used the Stooges' "Search and Destroy" in a 1996 television commercial, all bets were off. In recent years, Carnival Cruise Lines used music by Iggy Pop ("Lust for Life") while the Ramones ("Blitzkrieg Bop") sold Diet Pepsi. In 2008, former Sex Pistol John Lydon (aka Johnny Rotten) filmed a television commercial for Country Life butter, further damaging punk's anticapitalistic stance.

Film

The first documentaries about punks were made in the late 1970s by people within the punk scene. *Blank Generation,* a documentary shot by Ivan Kral (later guitarist for Patti Smith) and filmmaker Amos Poe, was one of the first to focus on the New York bands playing at CBGBs. Several influential and popular films made in England in the late 1970s captured well-known British punk bands in their prime. Don Letts' *The Punk Rock Movie* (1978), which featured the Clash and the Sex Pistols performing live, also included footage of the Heartbreakers with former New York Dolls Johnny Thunders and Jerry Nolan. Lech Kowalski's *D.O.A.* was primarily filmed on the Sex Pistols 1978 U.S. tour but included British bands Generation X and Sham 69 and American band the Dead Boys.

Just as it seemed American punk was fading, overshadowed by its British counterparts, Penelope Sphreeris' *Decline of Western Civilization* opened up Los Angeles punk to the rest of the world. Filmed between 1979 and 1981, the film captured the nascent Los Angeles hardcore scene and showcased the Germs, X, Black Flag, the Circle Jerks, and Fear.

By 1980, Hollywood studios sensed an opportunity, and feature films started to appear with punk characters and the requisite punk soundtrack. Robert Stigwood, producer of *Saturday Night Fever* and *Grease*, was one of the first with his *Times Square*, a contrived, awkward story of a rebellious punk girl in New York who teams up with a rich girl to (1) put together a band, (2) become famous for bizarre feats of vandalism, and (3) stick it to "the man." In the next few years, punk characters were introduced to the public in features such as *Ladies and Gentlemen, the Fabulous Stains* (1981), *Valley Girl* (1983), *Suburbia* (1984), and *Repo Man* (1984). While some films took a sincere and sympathetic look at the punk lifestyle (*Suburbia*) or evoked the punk world as a place where young people struggle for authenticity and self-expression (*The Fabulous Stains*), others portrayed punks as stereotypical antisocial deviants interested only in drugs, violence, and sex (*Class of 1984*).

Although few notable feature films have been made since 1990 that incorporate punk characters into the story, documentaries of varying quality are continually being released. Below are just a few of the many punk-related documentaries and feature films available:

Documentaries

Blank Generation (1976)—Excited by the new music coming out of lower Manhattan in the mid-1970s, Ivan Kral and Amos Poe used a Super 8 movie camera to shoot silent black and white footage of performances by the Ramones, Richard Hell, Patti Smith, Talking Heads, Blondie, Television, the Heartbreakers, and others at CBGBs. For the resulting film, they added unsynced live or demo recordings to their shaky, grainy footage, although in some cases the band obviously is not playing the song on the soundtrack. "Not having the synch on those films never bothered me," Poe said in 1978. "Because if you're in a real crazy club and there's a band on, half the time you can't see the whole band cause there's people all around. You see little parts of the band—a collage."[3] The resulting document is about as raw as many of these bands were in their early days.

D.O.A. (1980)—Lech Kowalski's documentary follows the Sex Pistols on their ill-fated 1978 U.S. tour that culminated in their show at San Francisco's Winterland Ballroom, their last show ever. Though essentially a look at British punk, the film provides a glimpse of American punks through interviews with Sex Pistols' fans across the United States. Most infamous for its interview with Sid Vicious and his girlfriend, Nancy Spungen, in their hotel room, the film also captures performances by the Dead Boys, the Clash, Sham 69, X-Ray Spex, Generation X, and others at their peak.

Decline of Western Civilization, Part I (1981)—An extremely important film in the history of American punk, Penelope Sphreeris' Decline, Part 1 (Parts 2 and 3 would follow) takes the viewer right into the heart of the Los Angeles punk scene to see where the bands play and live. Filmed over two years, she captures the end of the Hollywood punks and the beginning of hardcore as the audiences at shows were growing more aggressive and male. Her interviews with the disillusioned, angry white middle-class punks are still arresting thirty years later. She interviews the Germs singer Darby Crash as he tries to make breakfast (something she would repeat in Decline, Part 2 with Ozzy Osbourne) and sits down with Black Flag in their rehearsal space/living quarters in an abandoned church. Music critic Robert Palmer wrote: "The Decline is one of the sharpest and most exciting of all rock films, not because it captures society's death throes but because it captures a new generation of musicians and fans reinventing rock-and-roll."[4]

Another State of Mind (1983)—This engaging documentary of a self-planned and promoted 1982 U.S./Canadian tour by California bands Youth Brigade and Social Distortion was produced, written, and directed by Adam Small and Peter Stuart. As Youth Brigade's Shawn Stern described the tour, "We're just hoping to break even. We're not some big act that has a record company behind us doing everything for us. We're doing this all on our own independently. We're trying to prove to people that punks aren't some mindless morons who go around beating each other up and slashing each other like they say." Boarding an old school bus, the two bands and their roadies plan to play thirty to thirty-five shows over five weeks. The tour, a first for both groups, is a real eye-opener as they face unscrupulous concert promoters, disdain from local business people, and tight quarters and long hours on the bus. The film offers a close look at punks in various cities and the difficulties bands faced as they put the DIY philosophy into practice. According to filmmaker Stuart, "The whole purpose of the film wasn't to show punks as good or bad, but to highlight the diversity of the different scenes."[5]

End of the Century: Story of the Ramones (2003)—An insightful, heartfelt, and at times disturbing documentary of the dysfunctional faux family called the Ramones. Through interviews with all original band members and luminaries Eddie Vedder, Debby Harry, and former members of the Sex Pistols, filmmakers Michael Gramaglia and Jim Fields trace the lives of Joey, Johnny, Dee Dee, and their other counterparts from the late 1960s until the band's 2002 indoctrination into the Rock and Roll Hall of Fame and Dee Dee's death.

American Hardcore (2007)—Inspired by his book *American Hardcore: A Tribal History*, writer Steven Blush and director Paul Rachman take a look at the hardcore movement from 1978 to 1985. Traveling from Southern California and Washington, D.C., to Boston, New York, San Francisco, and elsewhere, the filmmakers interview all of the hardcore heavyweights about what attracted them to the scene. Amid snippets of performances from Bad Brains, Black Flag, Minor Threat, and dozens of other bands, the audience is reminded of what life was like under Ronald Reagan for many disillusioned, white, middle-class young people in the early 1980s. Unfortunately, the film doesn't attempt to explain who or what inspired the early hardcore pioneers, making it appear as if hardcore emerged out of nowhere, ginned up in the minds of Gregg Ginn (Black Flag) and H. R. (Bad Brains).

Punk's Not Dead (2007)—Using archival footage and recent interviews from a who's who of U.S. and British punk musicians, filmmaker Susan Dynner's insightful film looks at the state of punk circa 2006. The film offers a glimpse into the lives of aging punk bands (mostly British) that have been together since the late 1970s and uses pop punk bands Sum 41 and Good Charlotte as examples in her investigation of whether a commercially successful band can still be punk. Musicians and music critics grapple with and disagree about the oft-discussed topics of what constitutes punk and whether punk even still exists.

Feature Films

Ladies and Gentlemen, the Fabulous Stains (1981)—Directed by music producer Lou Adler for major film studio Paramount, *Ladies and Gentlemen, the Fabulous Stains* is not so much a punk rock movie as a cynical look at the music business, journalism, and aging rock and rollers. Now a cult hit, the film tells the story of Corinne Burns, an angry, sullen young woman in a small Pennsylvania town who forms a band with her sister and cousin. After three rehearsals, the Stains are asked to go on a rock and roll tour with the Looters, a punk group featuring ex–Sex Pistols Steve Jones and Paul Cook and the Clash's Paul Simenon, and the Metal Corpses, a group of poorly aging heavy metal stars. Corinne's brutal honesty and willingness to speak out against the limited prospects offered to young women endears her to the girls in the audience, who immediately begin emulating her look. Within days (this is a movie after all), the Stains accumulate hundreds of fans, hire a manager, get top billing on the show, and lose it all when fans rebel. The film includes four songs by Cook and Jones, who are seen performing "Join the Professionals."

Class of 1984 (1982)—Called "an intentionally camp exploitation feature" upon its release,[6] this violent story of a group of punks who terrorize a high school captures the age-old teenage battle against authority—only in this case, the rebellious youth are members of a small punk gang who sell and use drugs, disrupt classes, vandalize property, fight, and eventually rape the wife of a teacher, whom they also try to kill. Other than the lead punk, Peter Stegman, played by Timothy Van Patten, the punks never move beyond their antisocial caricatures. Directed by famed exploitation film director Mark Lester, *Class of 1984*'s low-budget style gives the film a gritty realism that became commonplace in independent films in the following two decades.

Smithereens (1982)—Made for $80,000 by twenty-nine-year-old Susan Seidelman, *Smithereens* follows Wren, a nineteen-year-old from

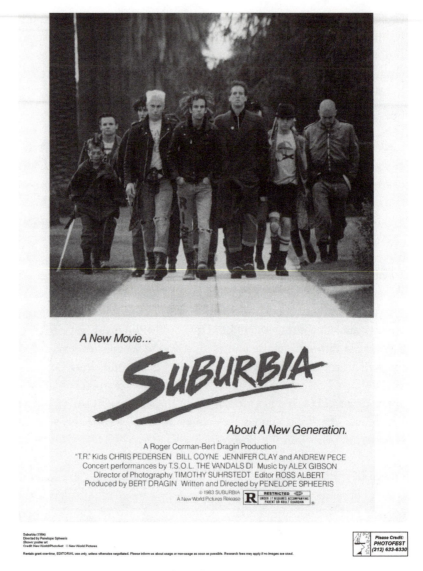

A New Movie...

SUBURBIA

About A New Generation.

A Roger Corman-Bert Dragin Production
"T.R." Kids CHRIS PEDERSEN BILL COYNE JENNIFER CLAY and ANDREW PECE
Concert performances by T.S.O.L. THE VANDALS DI Music by ALEX GIBSON
Director of Photography TIMOTHY SUHRSTEDT Editor ROSS ALBERT
Produced by BERT DRAGIN Written and Directed by PENELOPE SPHEERIS

© 1983 SUBURBIA
A New World Pictures Release

R RESTRICTED
UNDER 17 REQUIRES ACCOMPANYING
PARENT OR ADULT GUARDIAN

Suburbia (1984)
Directed by Penelope Spheeris
Shown: poster art
Credit: New World/Photofest © New World Pictures

Rentals grant one-time, EDITORIAL use only, unless otherwise negotiated. Please inform us about usage or non-usage as soon as possible. Research fees may apply if no images are used.

Please Credit:
PHOTOFEST
(212) 633-6330

Penelope Spheeris's 1984 film Suburbia *presented a realistic portrait of young punks trying to survive outside the system. (© New World Pictures, New World/Photofest.)*

New Jersey, as she searches for fame in lower Manhattan. In true punk style, Wren's lack of any discernible talent doesn't slow her down at all as she pastes up flyers of herself around town and talks up her plans with everyone she meets. Along the way she is kicked out of her apartment, lives in a van with Paul, a young man from Montana, and becomes infatuated with local star Eric, played by real-life punk icon Richard Hell. Shot on the streets and in the clubs and apartments of New York City, the film captures the noise, dirt, and feel of the city circa 1980. Seidelman's film was accepted into the Cannes Film Festival in France, a rare feat for an independent film in 1982.

Suburbia (1984)—Penelope Spheeris followed *The Decline of Western Civilization*, her documentary about the Los Angeles punk scene, with *Suburbia*, a film about a group of punks living together in an abandoned tract house in Los Angeles. Escaping from homes where they were abused or ignored, the punks band together, tattoo themselves T.R. (for The Rejected), and share communal responsibilities: foraging for food, panhandling, and protecting themselves from wild dogs and aggressive nonpunks who attack them from time to time. Spheeris based her script on stories she saw on the news and heard from young people, and she cast a number of people she met at punk shows, which gives the film an unusual air of authenticity. The film was widely praised and credited with providing one of the best examples of the harsh reality of these young people's lives. The *Washington Post* called it a "sobering, sensitive tale of runaway punks surviving in a blighted world."[7]

Repo Man (1984)—In Alex Cox's surrealist satire set in Southern California, Harry Dean Stanton stars as Bud, a man who repossesses automobiles and takes Otto, a young punk played by Emilio Estevez, under his wing to teach him the business. The film pokes fun at cults, televised religion, punk criminals, UFO believers, the CIA, generic food, and other segments of modern American life. When selecting it as one of the ten best films of the year, *Los Angeles Times* critic Sheila Benson called the film "fresh and virulently funny" and "probably the most inventive American movie of the year."[8] *Repo Man* features music by the Circle Jerks and the Untouchables (both in the film) as well as Black Flag and the Plugz.

What We Do Is Secret (2007)—Roger Grossman's film is a biopic of Los Angeles punk band the Germs with actor Shane West channeling lead singer Darby Crash. Whether he was a punk rock visionary or seriously overrated, Crash's short life had a profound effect on the people who knew him in the late 1970s. Although the film received mixed reviews, with the help of former Germ Pat Smear, the producers made a great effort to recreate the band's chaotic, violent performances and the Los Angeles punk scene as it looked and felt at that time.

NOTES

1. Hilburn, Robert, "The Menace and Charm of Punk Rock," *Los Angeles Times*, August 1, 1976, K72.
2. Safire, William. "Punk's 'Horror Show,'" *New York Times*, June 30, 1977, 19.
3. *Search and Destroy* magazine, 1978, 22.
4. Palmer, Robert. "Punk: Re-Forming Rock," *New York Times*, July 8, 1981, C21.
5. Goldstein, Patrick. "6 Hard Weeks in a Punk State of Mind," *Los Angeles Times*, October 28, 1983, G19.
6. Vincent Canby, "School Gang in 'Class of 1984,'" *New York Times*, August 21, 1982.
7. Harrington, Richard. "*Suburbia*—A Sobering, Sensitive Tale," *Washington Post*, February 11, 1984, G1.
8. Benson, Sheila. "Ten Best Film Picks—And Then Some," *Los Angeles Times*, December 30, 1984, J25.

CHAPTER SEVEN

Punk in the New Century

After three decades, punk lives on in America, but the scene has become so fragmented that it is difficult to find a dominant punk subculture amid the many offshoots. Although disparate groups have always jostled against each other within the punk community, some groups that began in the punk scene, such as emo, have been around so long that they have developed their own subcultures. Other subsets, like the anarcho-punks and gutter punks, have existed as small minorities for years and remain subsets of punk in general. There are also many people who are drawn to "pop punk," a pejorative term used by some punks and music critics to describe bands that play punk-style songs with catchy melodies. Many older punks believe the pop punk bands and their fans do not share punk's predominant anticapitalism or antiauthoritarianism ideals and should not even be called punk.

The relationship between punk and mainstream culture has evolved greatly since 1985, when a school ban on punk clothing and hairstyles in Minneapolis led 300 junior high school students to take to the streets, pound on cars, and trample across lawns. (School officials blamed punk clothing for being distracting and promoting mischievous behavior.) Punk is no longer the frightening, threatening subculture it once was. Old punk stars hawk products in commercials while classic

The Dropkick Murphys, an Irish–American punk band, perform with Irish step dancers before Game 7 of baseball's American League Championship Series on October 21, 2007, at Fenway Park in Boston. (AP Photo/Elise Amendola)

punk songs pop up in advertisements for cruise ships. In 2007, Irish-American punk band the Dropkick Murphys even performed with Irish step dancers at Boston's Fenway Park before Game 7 of baseball's American League Championship Series.

Over time, the markers that distinguished punk have become blurred as much of punk culture has been co-opted by the culture at large. Certainly punk's DIY approach to art, creativity, and business has been incorporated into everyday American life with inexpensive computer software allowing people to make films, record music, write books and fanzines, and promote their work online.

Even the term "punk" itself has been appropriated to sell products and services. Americans can participate in punk yoga, punk bowling, punk knitting, or buy books on punk marketing, punk science, and punk shui home design. Children can enjoy a book called *Punk Farm*.

Punk on the Web

Changes in technology have also changed the punk community. After the late 1990s, as print fanzines disappeared and radio shows began to broadcast online, the Internet became the primary gathering place for punks. Tens of thousands of punk-related Web sites of various quality are up and running, catering to all aspects and sub-genres of punk.

Although many of these online sites are commercial enterprises designed to sell clothing or music, others provide the community with valuable information and give punks a place to network, discuss issues, or read a little about punk history. Punknews.org, for example, began publishing in October 1999 to provide an inclusive community-based site where fans can read about and discuss punk, ska, hardcore, emo, metal, and indie music. The all-volunteer staff update the site daily. Punk radio stations abound on the Internet, featuring DJs from across the country playing punk from around the globe. Interviews with punk legends are available on podcasts. Extensive archives are housed online with information about bands, record labels, Web zines, record stores, and punk history. And, perhaps most importantly, declining subscriptions and increased costs have led to the demise of many beloved paper zines, including *Flipside*, *Punk Planet*, and *Suburban Voice*, though some, like Philadelphia's *Threatening Society* (TS), which published six issues in the mid-to-late 1980s, have been made available online.

Vital or Nostalgia?

Punk was a movement started by young people as a reaction to and rebellion against what they saw and disliked in society. Punks poured youthful energy into their music, which they drew from older musicians they admired while reshaping it into something new. By its very nature, punk rock is music by and for young people. That punk rockers would not grow old gracefully was a given. As they aged, some members of their audience may have moved away from punk, but a small subset aged with them, still ready to raise a middle finger to the hypocrisy and misguided values they find in politics, organized religion, and the corporate world.

In the new century, some punk pioneers refuse to fade into the shadows. Patti Smith and Iggy Pop, often described as the godmother and godfather of punk, still record and perform live without losing one bit of their edge. In 2003, Iggy re-formed his protopunk band the Stooges with original members Ron and Scott Asheton. After releasing one new album they toured, packing in crowds of young people as well as fans in their 40s and 50s. That the band had originally broken up in 1974, well before many of their audience had even been born, did not diminish the power of the ageless Pop fronting the tidal wave of primal rock pounded out by the band.

In 2005, influential protopunks the New York Dolls also reunited. With the two surviving original members—David Johansen and Sylvain Sylvain—and help from four new players, the band released *Some Day It Will Please Us to Remember Even This*, its first official recording since 1974's aptly named *Too Much, Too Soon*.

For many old and new fans alike, it was enough to hear Smith's "Gloria," the Stooges' "T.V. Eye," and the Dolls "Jet Boy" live on stage. While it's not the same as it would have been to hear these musicians in the 1970s when they were in their prime, their energy and attitude are still there, proving that punks can grow old and have some fun without destroying their legacy.

What Is Punk?

In a subculture that claims to value individual rights and thinking for oneself above all else, it should be no surprise that questions like "what is punk?" continue to provoke arguments.

In recent years, debate has raged among punks about whether someone can become commercially successful and still be punk. For years commercial success was not much of an issue for punks, but it became a hot topic in the 1990s, when punk groups started to sell a lot of records and tickets. To some, any cooperation with mainstream culture, including major record labels, corporate sponsorship, and merchandising, remain a sellout of punk's basic anticapitalist principles. Others, in particular musicians in bands who have suddenly found themselves commercially viable, maintain that the goal of punk is to open people's minds and get them to take action to improve the world. They argue that the more people they reach with their message, the better. Their goal was never to spend their lives playing in the garage to a handful of people.

Filmmaker Susan Dynner's 2007 film *Punk's Not Dead* looked at the state of punk circa 2005–2006 and asked musicians, both old-school and contemporary, whether punk was still alive. Not unexpectedly, the opinions varied—widely. Dynner chose to end the film with an optimistic conclusion that punk still exists and will always exist,

Punk Biographies

Billie Joe Armstrong (February 17, 1972–)

The lead singer, guitarist, and primary lyricist for Green Day, the first American punk band to attain huge mainstream success and the one credited for introducing punk music to a mass audience, Billie Joe Armstrong was born the youngest of six children in a working-class family and grew up in Rodeo, a small town fifteen miles north of Berkeley, California. Armstrong loved to sing and perform, even as a young child. At age eleven, he met fellow punk rock fan Mike Drint in school, and the two soon started playing music together. As teenagers, their band Sweet Children performed at parties around the San Francisco Bay area and at the Gilman Street Project, the long-lived all-ages club in Berkeley. The band eventually changed their name to Green Day after recording their first EP in 1989. The following year Armstrong dropped out of high school when Larry Livermore, founder of Lookout! Records, signed Green Day to record their first album, *39/Smooth*, which cost $675 to record. That November, when Green Day added drummer Tre Cool, their lineup was set. Their second album *Kerplunk* (Lookout!, 1992) was followed by their first major label release, *Dookie* (Reprise, 1994), featuring fast songs, catchy melodies, and lyrics that expressed teenage angst brought on by lone-liness and boredom. *Dookie* struck a chord with the public, skyrocket-ing the band to international stardom and selling millions of copies. Green Day inadvertently found themselves at the forefront of a group of new bands labeled "pop punk." Armstrong and his bandmates later released *Insomniac* (1995), *Nimrod* (1997), and *Warning* (2000), albums that sold well while garnering less attention than *Dookie*. Then, in 2004, their career took on a new dimension when they recorded their rock opera/concept album *American Idiot*, a scathing look at contem-porary American culture, which Armstrong believed had been co-opted by corporate greed and mass marketing. *American Idiot* was a tour de force, debuting at #1 on the Billboard charts and winning the 2005 Grammy Award for Best Rock Album. Some argue that this type of success is antithetical to punk, but Armstrong disagrees. In April 1998, he said: "Punk is not just the sound, the music. Punk is a lifestyle. There are a lot of bands around who claim to be punk and they only play the music, they have no clue what it's all about. It's a lifestyle I chose for myself. It's not about popularity and all that crap. We're just as much punk as we used to be."[1] In June 2009, the band put out their long-awaited follow-up, *21st Century Breakdown*. Like other famous rock stars, the band promoted the album widely on network television talk shows and *Saturday Night Live* and began a tour of U.S. and European sports arenas. Armstrong, married to Adrianne Nesser since 1994, has two children and lives in Northern California.

NOTE

1. New York Rock. "Billie Joe Armstrong of Green Day Interview." www.nyrock .com/interviews/greenday.htm.

Tim Armstrong (November 25, 1966–)

The leader of Rancid, one of the most successful punk bands of the 2000s, and the founder of Hellcat Records, a label dedicated to ska punk music, Tim Armstrong grew up in Northern California listening to the Ramones and the Clash. In 1987, he founded his first significant band, the ska-punkers Operation Ivy, which lasted just two years and released one EP and one influential album. Two years later, Armstrong started Rancid with bassist and childhood friend Matt Freeman. With drummer Brett Reed on board, they released their first EP the following year and their first album, *Rancid*, on the Epitaph label in 1993. After the success of *Let's Go*, their sophomore effort, and their first with guitarist Lars Frederiksen, the band was pursued by several major record labels but chose to stay with Epitaph even after finding widespread success. Their third album ... *And Out Come the Wolves*, with its three singles, "Roots Radicals," "Time Bomb," and "Ruby Soho," was a massive hit and was awarded a gold record for sales exceeding 500,000 copies. In 2003 Rancid finally signed with a major record label, Warner Brothers, and put out *Indestructible*, a Top 20 hit. A review in *Blender* magazine called *Indestructible* "a great record" and claimed, "Six albums on, Rancid seem as permanent as uranium. Some punk bands sound savage. Rancid sound happy they found punk rock, which saved them from a life of dead-end jobs and assorted addictions."[1] After a hiatus that began in 2004, the band reunited for a tour in 2006 but would not record a new album until 2009's *Let the Dominoes Fall*, the band's first album without their original lineup. Drummer Brett Reed left the band in 2006 and was replaced by Branden Steineckert, former drummer and founding member of the Used. Armstrong maintains an active musical life outside of Rancid. He released two albums between 2002 and 2005 with the Transplants; produced a number of records for artists such as Pink, Lars Frederiksen and the Bastards, F-Minus, and the Matches; put out a solo album, *The Poet's Life* (2007); and continues to work as talent scout for Hellcat Records, a subsidiary label of Epitaph.

NOTE

1. Blender, "Rancid Indestructible Review." www.blender.com/guide/new/51742/indestructible.html.

Jello Biafra (born Eric Boucher, June 17, 1958–)

Musician, political activist, and spoken-word artist Jello Biafra formed the punk group Dead Kennedys with East Bay Ray and Klaus Flouride in San Francisco in 1978. They played their first show on July 19 after rehearsing only one week. The following year, the band released its first single, "California Über Alles," and toured the East Coast. Among the most political hardcore bands in the country, Biafra ran for mayor of San Francisco in 1979, eventually coming in fourth out of ten candidates and forcing a runoff. After the band's first album, *Fresh Fruit for Rotting Vegetables*, with "Holiday in Cambodia" and "Kill the Poor," was released in 1980, they became the first U.S. punk band without a major record label to tour Europe and England. Biafra used his newly created record label, Alternative Tentacles, to promote hardcore by releasing a compilation album, *Let Them Eat Jellybeans*, with tracks by Black Flag, DOA, Flipper, Bad Brains, and Half Japanese. The Kennedys followed their next single, "Too Drunk to F***," with "Nazi Punks F*** Off" from the *In God We Trust, Inc.*, EP in late 1981. Biafra continued to release music from new bands, including TSOL, Hüsker Dü, Bad Brains, and DOA, enabling some hardcore bands to set up their own nationwide tours. But Biafra's success as a well-known provocateur soon landed him in legal trouble. *Frankenchrist*, the Dead Kennedy's 1985 album, contained a poster by Swiss artist H.R. Giger entitled *Landscape #XX*, an image composed of penises and vulvas. Three months after Biafra gave his first spoken-word performance in January 1986, police raided his house, carting away copies of *Frankenchrist* and the offending poster. The band, charged with distributing harmful material to minors, became entangled in legal proceedings that lasted more than a year and eventually ended in a hung jury. But the trial and its media frenzy had taken a toll, leading to the end of the Dead Kennedys and Biafra's marriage. Biafra began anew as a spoken-word artist and, along with his occasional musical collaborations with Ministry's Al Jourgenson (several albums under the name Lard), Mojo Nixon (a roots rock and country album called *Prairie Home Invasion*), the Melvins, and others, has remained a political activist. He debated political and social issues on television's *Crossfire*, *Donahue*, and the *Oprah Winfrey Show*, and in 2000, the New York State Green Party drafted him as a candidate for the Green Party's presidential nomination.

Rodney Bingenheimer (December 15, 1947–)

One of the best-known disc jockeys in America, Rodney Bingenheimer used his influential radio show on Los Angeles' KROQ-FM station to introduce listeners to untold numbers of new punk groups. Beginning in 1976, "Rodney on the ROQ" was in the forefront, playing Blondie, the Ramones, the Sex Pistols, the Cramps, the Clash, X, Bad Religion, the Jam, the Runaways, Redd Kross, Joan Jett, L7, Sonic Youth, Nirvana, the Strokes, the Hives, the Vines, and Black Rebel Motorcycle Club, usually before other radio shows picked them up. Bingenheimer had a long career on the fringes of the music industry. In the early 1970s, he helped David Bowie get a contract with RCA records, wrote national music columns for magazines, and operated and co-owned his club, "Rodney Bingenheimer's English Disco." There he played glam rock music and socialized with Iggy Pop, Led Zeppelin, Elton John, and other rock stars who happened to drop by. He was eventually nicknamed Mayor of the Sunset Strip for his many connections in the music business. In the 1980s, he heavily promoted new bands such as the Germs and Black Flag and between 1980 and 1982 released three "Rodney on the ROQ" albums featuring California hardcore and punk bands. A 2003 documentary, *Mayor of the Sunset Strip*, looked at Bingenheimer's life and long-lived radio show, which he still uses to introduce his audience to new rock and roll.

Greg Ginn (June 8, 1954–)

Greg Ginn founded the legendary Southern California hardcore band Black Flag and launched SST Records, one of the preeminent U.S. hardcore labels. Black Flag began in 1977 in Hermosa Beach, about twenty miles south of Los Angeles, with Ginn playing guitar and writing the band's songs, as he would through numerous lineup changes over the next ten years. The initial group featured singer Keith Morris, who left in 1979 to start the Circle Jerks, bassist Gary McDaniel (later known as Chuck Dukowski), and drummer Robo. Delays in getting their first EP released prompted Ginn to found SST Records in January 1979 and put out the band's *Nervous Breakdown* EP himself. After Morris departed, singer Ron Reyes and then Dez Cadena joined as the band's reputation grew. Their audiences' violent clashes with police during their shows brought the group a steady barrage of negative press from mainstream Southern California media. Police surveillance and harassment increased, and the band's shows were often shut down. When Cadena moved to guitar, Ginn brought superfan Henry Garfield (later Henry Rollins) on board to sing. With this lineup, they recorded their classic *Damaged* album in 1981. By 1984 the band had gone through a number of musical changes that led to the longer, slower, more experimental material captured on the *My War* LP. Workaholic Ginn drove the band on through marathon rehearsals and relentless touring, and after firing bassist Kira Roessler, one of the few women to play in a hardcore band at the time, Ginn broke up Black Flag in 1986. He later released solo albums and worked with the bands Gone and Comfort James while still running SST, which had previously released music by the Minutemen, Hüsker Dü, Bad Brains, and Sonic Youth. Considered by some the most influential guitarist to come out of the hardcore scene, Ginn continues to record and perform. In the late 1990s he said, "I feel lucky that I have never had to pick up a guitar or bass and play something I didn't want to play. I never wanted to be a musician, I just wanted to play music—my own music."[1] In September 2003 he pulled together a Black Flag reunion show, minus its most famous members, to benefit cat rescue. As Rollins said about his former bandmate in 1997, "I'm in awe of that guy. I think he is the man. I have never been on the stage with anybody that is that electrifying. Once in a lifetime do guys like that go across the horizon."[2]

NOTES

1. Sinker, Daniel, ed. *We Owe You Nothing* (New York: Akashic Books, 2001), 83.
2. Ibid., 88.

Brett Gurewitz (May 12, 1962–)

A founding member of the long-lasting Southern California punk band Bad Religion, Brett Gurewitz started and manages the independent music label, Epitaph. Gurewitz grew up in Woodland Hills in the San Fernando Valley just north of Los Angeles. In high school he met bandmates Greg Graffin, Jay Ziskrout, and Jay Bentley, and in 1982 they released their first full-length album, *How Could Hell Be Any Worse?*, financed in part by Gurewitz's father. After their second album, Gurewitz left the band but rejoined again in 1987. Their subsequent release, *Suffer* (1988), provided a watershed moment in punk history as the first melodic hardcore album. Gurewitz left Bad Religion again after the 1994 release of their highly acclaimed album *Stranger Than Fiction* to ostensibly concentrate on running Epitaph, which had produced a hit record with the

Offspring's *Smash*. Epitaph took off as Gurewitz put out records by popular 1990's punk bands NOFX, Rancid, and Pennywise. Yet despite his
success, Gurewitz retreated deeper into his on-again, off-again heroin
addiction. He and his wife, Maggie, divorced in 1995 and for a while his
life was marked by drug addiction, periods in rehab, arrests for drug pos-
session, an overdose, and time in jail. After finally getting clean, he
rejoined Bad Religion in 2001 before they recorded *The Process of Belief*
(2002), though he does not tour with the band. Gurewitz, who remarried
in 2004, continues to run Epitaph, which has grown into one of the
biggest independent labels in the world: the label and its subsidiaries have
released records by Agnostic Front, Joe Strummer and the Mescaleros,
Tom Waits, Guttermouth, Descendents, and many others. He signs and
produces new bands and still works on new material for Bad Religion.

Kathleen Hanna (November 12, 1968–)

Co-founder of the band Bikini Kill, Kathleen Hanna was one of the originators of the Riot Grrrl movement in the early 1990s and eventually
became the voice and face of Riot Grrrl in the media. From a young age,
the Bethesda, Maryland, native had been interested in feminist issues.
While attending college in Olympia, Washington, in the late 1980s,
Hanna used photography and spoken-word performances to explore sexism and worked to create a feminist art gallery, Reko Muse. With Tobi
Vail, who produced the *Jigsaw* zine and played drums, she developed a
zine called *Revolution Girl Style Now*. Next up, she created the *Bikini Kill*
zine with Kathi Wilcox, which took on sexism in the punk rock scene. In
1990, Hanna asked Vail and Wilcox to form a band, Bikini Kill. From the
outset, the band's songs challenged gender inequality, sexism, and violence through Hanna's confrontational and extremely personal lyrics. The
band moved to Washington, D.C., in 1991 with their new guitarist Billy
Karren. Together with members of the all-female band Bratmobile and a
few other women, Hanna and Vail started the *Riot Grrrl* zine and movement by setting up weekly meetings where women would discuss skills
sharing—creating fanzines, playing instruments, and putting on shows.
In 2003 Hanna said, "The whole idea [of Riot Grrrl] was that women
and girls could define what it meant and that there are a million different
ways to be feminist or womanist or to be prowoman or antimisogyny and
that it's not one person who can decide that. We didn't want to be a cor-

poration with a mission statement."[1] Bikini Kill released its first recording, a self-titled EP produced by Ian MacKaye, in 1991 on the Kill Rock Stars label. Over the next five years, the band put out several more records. Hanna then moved to Portland, Oregon, and worked on several musical projects, including Julie Ruin, a solo venture. In 1996, she married Adam Horovitz of the hip-hop group Beastie Boys and later moved to New York City. There, Hanna, along with zine writer and artist Johanna Fateman and musician/video artist Sadie Benning, started Le Tigre, a dance/punk band focused on feminist and queer-friendly issues. The band put out three albums, with JD Sampson stepping in after Benning left in 2001. In 2007 the band went on hiatus.

NOTE

1. http://ladieslotto.blogspot.com/2008/03/kathleen-hanna-womens-history-month.html.

Richard Hell (born Richard Meyers, October 2, 1949–)

Leader of the 1970s punk band Richard Hell and the Voidoids, cofounder of two seminal New York punk bands—Television and the Heartbreakers—and the first person credited with adopting the spiky hair and safety pin look of early punk, Richard Hell was raised in Lexington, Kentucky, but dropped out of high school in 1966 and moved to New York City. With an eye to making his name as a poet, Hell bought a used table-top offset printing press and began publishing books and magazines. His poems were also published in periodicals ranging from *Rolling Stone* to the *New Directions Annuals*. In 1973, Hell and his best friend from high school, Tom Miller (later Tom Verlaine), started their first rock band, the Neon Boys. The band eventually evolved into Television, the first rock band to perform at CBGBs. Of those days, Hell says,

> We didn't think of ourselves or refer to ourselves as "punk" musicians but rather as ones who knew what we wanted to try to do in music, which was change the way rock 'n' roll was being played at the time and change general attitudes towards kids' music bands and what they meant and what they could do. What I wanted was for music to be about real life again, which the pop music at the time was not, and to me real life seemed dirty and crazy and intense as well as funny.[1]

After disputes with Verlaine, Hell left the band in 1975 and formed the Heartbreakers with two ex–New York Dolls, guitarist Johnny Thunders and drummer Jerry Nolan. The following year he assembled the Voidoids, who were quickly signed to Sire Records. The title track of their first album, *Blank Generation* (1977), soon became an early punk anthem. Hell was a sporadic musician/performer and rarely played outside of New York City, his interest in traveling curtailed in part by a severe heroin addiction. His follow-up album, *Destiny Street*, was not released until 1982. Although he retired from music in the mid-1980s to concentrate on writing, in 1992 he joined Thurston Moore and Steve Shelley of Sonic Youth and Don Fleming of Gumball to record a one-off CD, *Dim Stars*. Since then Hell has written two novels—*Go Now* (1996) and *Godlike* (2005)—poetry, numerous film reviews, and assorted other articles. Though he claims he's not part of the punk culture, he says he does "like and identify with the kind of independence and antiauthoritarianism and do-it-yourself [rather than bend to corporate values] works, such as can be found in comics, zines, independent filmmaking, local bands, and artist-run labels, etc.," but to him it's all personal: "I don't have much faith or belief, or [most of all] interest in alternative societies or alternative belief systems," he says.[2]

NOTES

1. Richard Hell Official Site. "My Punk Beginnings & Are Rock Lyrics Poetry?" www.richardhell.com/punkpoetry.html.
2. Ibid.

John Holmstrom (1954–)

Illustrator John Holmstrom founded *Punk* magazine with Legs McNeil and Ged Dunn in New York City in late 1975. The magazine, the first to focus on the new bands playing at CBGBs, introduced the term "punk rock" to wider audiences. "Punk was a dirty word at the time," Holmstrom said. "Us putting 'punk' on the cover was like putting the word f*** on the cover."[1] Holmstrom had attended New York's School of Visual Arts (SVA) where he studied under Will Eisner, legendary illustrator and the creator of the graphic novel, and worked as an assistant for Harvey Kurtzman, who created the original *Mad* magazine. With their guidance, Holmstrom eventually developed his iconic style that would become the look of early punk graphics. After dropping out of school in 1974, Holmstrom and McNeil, both fans of the band the Dictators, began hanging out at CBGBs where they met and interviewed Lou Reed and the Ramones for the first issue of *Punk*. For the next four years, the magazine combined Holmstrom's drawings with McNeil's wacky interviews and Mary Harron, Roberta Bayley, and Bob Gruen's stories and photos to capture the look, irreverence, and humor of the early punk movement. Holmstrom's style fit most closely with the Ramones' image and in 1978 he drew the back cover of their *Rocket to Russia* album. The following year he illustrated the front cover of their fourth album, *Road to Ruin*. From 1976 to 1979, Holmstrom published fifteen issues of *Punk* before financial problems forced him to shut down the magazine, even though he was printing 25,000 copies of each issue. After *Punk* folded, Holmstrom struggled to make a living as an illustrator, drawing covers for *Screw* and *Village Voice* and records by alternative bands. By 1986, Holmstrom had begun working for *High Times* magazine, first as an editor and then as its publisher. He left the magazine in 2000 to revive *Punk* for its twenty-fifth anniversary and still puts out intermittent issues.

NOTE

1. Heylin, Clinton. *From the Velvets to the Voidoids* (New York: Penguin Books, 1993), 242.

Hilly Kristal (September 23, 1931–August 28, 2007)

Hilly Kristal owned CBGBs, the legendary New York City punk club, ground zero for the New York punk scene in the 1970s. Kristal had a long background in music, studying the violin and opera as a child and later attending the Settlement Music School in Philadelphia. He then moved to New York City and began a career in music, singing in the men's chorus at Radio City Music Hall before managing the Village Vanguard Jazz Club in Greenwich Village, where he booked Miles Davis and other jazz luminaries. After spending several years booking folk and jazz acts in other New York City clubs, he opened his own club, Hilly's, in 1966 in the Bowery, a crime-ridden area in lower Manhattan. In 1973, he opened CBGB-OMFUG (Country, Bluegrass, Blues, and Other Music for Uplifting Gourmandizers), and within a year began booking new unsigned local acts. Famously, he did not care if or how well bands played their instruments—but they had to write their own songs. Cover bands were banned. By late 1974, his club was the center of the burgeoning New York punk scene. Singer Patti Smith, one of the first to play on his stage, called Kristal "the good shepherd of a flock of black sheep."[1] In the 1980s and 1990s, Kristal booked hardcore punk bands, began a hardcore matinee show on Sunday afternoons, and opened a gallery, record store, and fashion line. For thirty-two years, Kristal ran CBGBs, until exorbitant rent increases forced him to close in October 2006. "[CBGBs] has a lot of good meaning for people: of getting together, of playing music together," he said. "You know it's a very good thing we need these days."[2] Kristal died from lung cancer in August 2007. CBGBs continues to sell clothing, accessories, and CDs online and in its New York City store.

NOTES

1. *New York Sun.* "Hilly Kristal, 75, Began CBGB, Home of Punk," by Stephen Miller. www.nysun.com/obituaries/hilly-kristal-75-began-cbgb-home-of-punk/ 61613/.
2. Ibid.

Larry Livermore (born Lawrence Hayes, 1947–)

Cofounder of Lookout! Records, Larry Livermore recorded a number of San Francisco Bay area punk bands beginning in the late 1980s. In 1985, Livermore founded, sang, and played guitar in the Lookouts with a twelve-year-old drummer, Tre Cool, who later joined Green Day. The band released two albums and two EPs over the next five years on Lookout! Records, a label Livermore started with David Hayes, in part to document some of the bands performing at the Gilman Street Project in Berkeley. In the next decade, the label released records by ska punk bands Operation Ivy and Rancid and many other new bands, including Green Day and the Queers, who would later bring punk music to a new generation of teenagers. Livermore also wrote for his label's fanzine, *Lookout!*, wrote regular columns for *Maximum Rocknroll*, and from 1994 to 2007 contributed a monthly column to *Punk Planet* magazine. In 1997, Livermore retired from Lookout! Records, a move he attempted to explain in 2009:

> I hardly ever meet anyone from the music scene who doesn't ask me some version of 'Why did you leave Lookout[!]?' and I don't think I've yet succeeded in delivering a reasonable answer, either to them or myself. . . . Just as I had no idea how big and how rapidly Lookout! would grow when we started it in 1987, I had no idea how quickly those magic moments would pass and how much I would miss them when they were gone.[1]

Livermore continues to write articles and blogs.

NOTE

1. Larry Livermore.com. "Leaving Lookout." February 16, 2009. http://larrylivermore .blogspot.com.

Kevin Lyman (dates unavailable)

Kevin Lyman is the founder of the longest-running rock festival, the Vans Warped Tour, which has criss-crossed the United States, bringing punk from California to Massachusetts, since 1994. Along with numerous stages, the festival features a half-pipe for skaters and bikers, tents for bands to sell merchandise, and booths for independent record labels, magazine publishers, nonprofit organizations, and sponsors to market their products or message. Lyman began booking and promoting concerts in college and later became production manager for independent concert promoter Goldenvoice, where he worked with the Germs, Metallica, Circle Jerks, Anthrax, and Jane's Addiction. After three years' experience on the Lollapalooza traveling summer festival, in 1994 Lyman took a group of bands, including Sublime and No Doubt, on the road, an experience that turned into the Warped Tour in 1995. From the beginning, Lyman asked Vans, a company that manufactures sneakers, BMX shoes, and other footwear aimed at the skateboarder and surfer crowd, to sponsor the tour. His willingness to accept corporate sponsorship has been a continuing source of controversy for some in the punk community who believe corporations are antithetical to punk. Lyman responds,

> F*** corporate America was the motto of the day when I was working in the clubs. Then I thought, we spend money in corporate America why don't I try to go get some of this. [Corporations] are going to sell to you anyhow even though you don't think you're buying it. I'm going to use some of the money and at least give kids a great day with some of the money.[1]

In 2005, Lyman and John Reese started the winter Taste of Chaos tour, which later spun off an international version, and in 2008 he established the Mayhem Festival of metal bands. Lyman is also part owner of Side One Dummy Record Company, whose roster includes Irish band Flogging Molly, Anti-Flag, Royal Crown Review, the Mighty Mighty Bosstones, and others. The label also releases an annual compilation of songs by groups on that year's Warped Tour, which continues to play an essential role in American punk by introducing young bands to new audiences. "It's going to be weird the summer I don't have Warped Tour, to be honest," he said. "It's like that job—the year I die is the year I don't do Warped Tour. It will be predicated by when the kids stop coming, but I think it's a very important part of our music scene, and that's why the scene is pretty strong."[2]

NOTES

1. *Punk's Not Dead*, DVD, directed by Susan Dynner, 2007.
2. http://punkmusic.about.com/od/interviews/a/kevinlyman_2.htm.

Ian MacKaye (April 16, 1962–)

The former singer for Washington, D.C.-based bands Minor Threat and Fugazi and cofounder of Dischord Records with Jeff Nelson, Ian MacKaye is one of the most important and consistent voices in the punk community. A strong believer in the do-it-yourself ethic and a

Hardcore band Minor Threat (left to right, Brian Baker, Jeff Nelson, a fan, Ian MacKaye, Lyle Pressler) perform, January 1981. (© Athena Angelos. Used by permission.)

lifelong advocate for refraining from drugs, alcohol, and indiscriminate sexual encounters, MacKaye wrote the songs "Out of Step" and "Straight Edge," which inspired the straight-edge movement, although MacKaye never saw himself as part of that movement. As a teenager in Washington, D.C., MacKaye was inspired to start a band after attending an early show by the Cramps and was further influenced by local legends Bad Brains. When his first band, the Teen Idles, made a record, the group took the $600 they had saved and recorded and released an eight-song EP in November 1980—the first Dischord Records release. By the time the record came out, the band had broken up, so MacKaye formed Minor Threat with Nelson (drums), Lyle Pressler (guitar), and Brian Baker (bass). Despite their short lifespan and limited recorded legacy (twenty-six songs), Minor Threat became one of the most influential hardcore bands of all time. To accommodate their young fans, many still in high school, MacKaye arranged all-ages shows at local clubs. By putting an X on the backs of their hands, a sign that they would not drink, underage punks could come into clubs to listen to the music. The X became a symbol for the straight-edge movement that soon developed in Boston and New York. Through his bands Minor Threat, Embrace, and Fugazi, MacKaye remained true to his principles, advocating for causes ranging from female equality to vegetarianism to anticapitalism. From 1987 to 2001, as Fugazi's popularity grew, MacKaye insisted on keeping door prices low, refused to sell band merchandise, and turned down offers for interviews in publications that accepted advertising for alcohol or cigarettes. The band released seven albums and toured the world, always requiring that their shows be open to all ages. In 2001, with Fugazi on an indefinite hiatus, MacKaye formed the Evens, a duo with drummer Amy Farina. While the Evens record and tour, MacKaye continues to run Dischord Records.

Brendan Mullen (October 9, 1949–October 12, 2009)

Brendan Mullen founded the Masque, the first punk club in Hollywood, California, in the basement of an old building off Hollywood Boulevard in 1977. By hosting no-cover, all-ages shows featuring new bands such as the Bags, the Screamers, and the Weirdos, Mullen gave a new generation of bands a place to play and the budding Los Angeles punk scene a place to grow. After struggling to get punks to pay to see music, and after the police and fire marshals closed his club several times, Mullen held a Save the Masque Benefit in February 1978. But it was not enough, and Mullen eventually closed the club the following year. He spent the next two years trying to make a living as an independent promoter for punk shows, an experience that left him broke and homeless. In 1981, after working as a DJ for Club Lingerie on Sunset Boulevard, Mullen became the club's in-house booker, a position he held for eleven years. From 1986 to 1988, he also booked shows at the Variety Arts Center, a five-story complex in downtown Los Angeles. Throughout the 1980s, Mullen brought some of the best punk and alternative bands to Los Angeles' stages: Black Flag, Bad Brains, Hüsker Dü, the Butthole Surfers, Lydia Lunch, Sonic Youth, Redd Kross, Hole, and Jane's Addiction. He was also the first person in Los Angeles to book the Replacements, R.E.M., Soundgarden, and the Flaming Lips. In addition, Mullen has written several books: *We Got the Neutron Bomb* (2001), an overview of early Los Angeles punk (co-author Mark Spitz); *Lexicon Devil* (2002), a history of Darby Crash and the Germs (co-authors Don Bolles and Adam Parfrey); *Whores* (2006), an oral biography of Jane's Addiction; and *Live at the Masque: Nightmare in Punk Alley* (2007).

Iggy Pop (born James Osterberg, April 21, 1947–)

Iggy Pop and his band the Stooges were undeniably one of the major influences on punk music, leading him to be called the "godfather of punk." From the first few seconds of their 1969 self-titled debut, the band's coarse sound, with its distorted guitars and basic—even simplistic—chord changes and Iggy's bratty sneer, laid out a template that would be repeated by punk bands for decades. Songs from their three albums, *The Stooges* (1969), *Funhouse* (1970), and *Raw Power* (1973) have been covered by the Damned, Rage Against the Machine, the Dictators, Joan Jett, Everclear, and countless others. The Sex Pistols ended their final show with the Stooges' "No Fun." Iggy's showmanship—throwing himself around the stage, cutting himself with broken glass, and smearing peanut butter on his chest—has since been copied repeatedly. Iggy was born in Michigan and raised in a mobile home park outside of Ann Arbor, forty miles west of Detroit. In high school, he began playing the drums and started his first band, the Iguanas, at age fifteen. He later joined the Prime Movers, a local blues band. After a short stint in Chicago playing the blues, Iggy returned home and looked up guitar player Ron Asheton and Ron's brother Scott, a drummer. Together they formed the Psychedelic Stooges and played their first show on Halloween night 1967. With Dave Alexander on bass, the Stooges began performing at the Grande Ballroom in Detroit, often with the area's top rock band, the MC5. The Stooges' stage shows immediately excited audiences: Iggy appeared wearing white face paint and a maternity gown, jumped into the crowd, and gyrated wildly. The audience didn't know what to expect, but they loved it. In 1968, future Ramones manager Danny Fields signed both the MC5 and the Stooges to recording contracts. The following June, the Stooges recorded their first album in just two days with former Velvet Underground member John Cale producing. When it was released, music critic Ed Ward wrote, "Their music is loud, boring, tasteless, unimaginative and childish. I kind of like it."[1] By the time they recorded their follow-up, *Funhouse*, music papers across the country were writing about Iggy's self-destructive tendencies, from pouring hot wax on his chest to hitting himself with the microphone. As the band went through several lineup changes, Iggy, drummer Scott, and new guitarist James Williamson all became addicted to heroin. Unable to continue touring with his growing addiction, Iggy left the band in 1971. While he underwent a methadone program, the not-yet-famous

David Bowie persuaded his management company to get Iggy a record deal, and in early 1972, the Stooges traveled to London and recorded *Raw Power*, called by *Creem* magazine's Dave Marsh "the best album of the 1970's."[2] The album failed to sell, Bowie's management company dropped them, and drugs once again took over the group's life. Iggy left the Stooges again and moved with Bowie to Berlin, where they recorded *The Idiot* (1977) and *Lust for Life* (1977), two of his most memorable solo albums. From that point forward, his career careened from hard-driving records like *Instinct* (1988) and *American Caesar* (1993) to misfires like *Avenue B* (1999), a predominantly spoken-word album. Although Iggy's story has often been an "account of snatching defeat from the jaws of victory" as Bowie once said,[3] over the years his stature as one of rock's great showmen has grown while the Stooges' albums continue to inspire new generations of young musicians. In 2003 Iggy and Ron and Scott Asheton re-formed the Stooges for a tour that was followed in 2007 by their first album together since 1975, *The Weirdness*. Ron Asheton was found dead on January 6, 2009, from an apparent heart attack. Iggy Pop carries on.

NOTES

1. Rolling Stone, "The Stooges Album Review." www.rollingstone.com/reviews/album/227140/review/5941759/the_stooges.
2. Marsh, Dave. *Creem* magazine, March 1973.
3. Pop, Iggy, and Anne Wehrer. *I Need More*. (New York: Karz-Cohl Publishing, Inc., 1982), back cover.

The Ramones

Dee Dee Ramone (born Douglas Colvin, September 18, 1952–June 5, 2002), Joey Ramone (born Jeffrey Hyman, May 19, 1952–April 15, 2001), Johnny Ramone (born John Cummings, October 8, 1951–September 15, 2004), and Tommy Ramone (born Tommy Edrelyi, January 29, 1952–) were both one of the most original bands in the history of rock and roll and one of the most influential punk bands of all time. Even before they played their first shows, this foursome from the Forest Hills area of Queens, New York, had created a concept for their band that they would never change: four skinny guys named Ramone wearing ripped jeans and leather jackets and playing short, fast songs, many under two minutes long. They came to epitomize the initial look and sound of punk and the idea that a person didn't have to be a great musician to play in a rock band. They had energy and attitude—they did what they did and didn't care if people liked it or not. The Ramones first performed live in March 1974 and played their first show at New York's CBGBs in August, where they somehow managed to fit in among the more artsy bands such as Television and the Patti Smith Group. Of all of the early CBGBs bands, the Ramones were the most basic and the easiest to identify later as "punk." Some found the group hilarious, others were dumbfounded, and a few fell in love. "They looked perfect, sounded perfect, stood perfect, the songs were perfect," said Danny Fields who later managed the band. "The show was over in 11-and-a-half minutes. I was swept away."[1] Signed by Sire Records, the band recorded their first album, *The Ramones*, for just $6,200 and released it in April 1976. The album was in a league of its own: the fourteen songs clocked in at under thirty minutes, there were no guitar solos, and the harmonies and backing vocals were lifted straight from surf music of the early 1960s. "We thought the Ramones were going to be like the Beatles," says John Holmstrom, editor of *Punk* magazine. "We thought as soon as everyone heard their record, everyone would love them and they'd sell a million records." But—not surprisingly—the general public, busy buying *Frampton Comes Alive* and *The Eagles' Greatest Hits, 1971–1975*, weren't interested. Some critics, though, understood what was happening. Paul Nelson wrote in *Rolling Stone* magazine:

> Their first album, *Ramones*, is constructed almost entirely of rhythm tracks of an exhilarating intensity rock and roll has not experienced since its earliest days. The Ramones' lyrics are so compressed that there is no room for even one establishing atmosphere verse or one dramatically irrelevant guitar solo in which the musicians could suggest an everyday existence . . .[2]

Drummer Tommy left the band in 1978 and was replaced by Marky Ramone (born Mark Bell, July 15, 1956). Marky lasted until 1983, was replaced by Richie Ramone, and then returned in 1987. Many thought the band was through when bassist Dee Dee, one of the principal songwriters, left the group in 1989 and was replaced by C. J. Ramone. But they soldiered on for another seven years of almost continual touring and intermittent record releases. The Ramones are reported to have performed 2,263 concerts between 1974–1996 and to have released twenty-one studio, live, and compilation albums. In 2001, Joey Ramone died of lymphatic cancer. The following March, the band that never had a hit record was inducted into the Rock and Roll Hall of Fame. That June, Dee Dee Ramone, who had a well-documented history of drug addiction, died of an apparent overdose, and Johnny Ramone died after a fight with prostate cancer in 2004. The Ramones legacy lives on in bands such as Green Day, who openly acknowledge their debt to the four "brothers" from Queens.

NOTES

1. Blake, Mark, ed. *Punk: The Whole Story* (New York: DK Publishing, 2008), 52.
2. Nelson, Paul. "The Ramones," *Rolling Stone*, www.rollingstone.com/artists/ theramones/albums/album/158517/review/5946887/ramones_1st_lp.

Lou Reed (March 2, 1942–)

Considered one of the forefathers of punk for his groundbreaking work with the Velvet Underground in the 1960s and his willingness to write and record music with little regard for commercial success, Lou Reed was revered by many in the early New York punk scene for his songs about the gritty reality of life in the city. Reed never played punk music but was an icon to many who did. He was a legendary figure in New York by the time he was on the first cover of *Punk* magazine in January 1976. Reed was born in Freeport, Long Island, and by the time he was fourteen, he had formed his first band and released his first record. He graduated from Syracuse University with a degree in art and worked for a short time as an in-house songwriter for Pickwick Records before meeting violist John Cale, who had studied classical music in London. In 1965, with guitarist Sterling Morrison and drummer Maureen Tucker, they formed the Velvet Underground. Famed celebrity and artist Andy Warhol, an early supporter of the band, helped raise their visibility and pushed them to add a female singer, Nico. Reed eventually relented, and their first album was entitled, *The Velvet Underground and Nico*. Released in 1966 during the height of the flower power days, the album did not sell well with its songs like "I'm Waiting for the Man," about a drug buy, "Venus in Furs," about an S&M relationship, and "The Black Angel's Death Song," featuring Cale's viola squawking furiously behind Reed's monotone recitation. The album, now considered one of the most influential records of all time, came in at #13 on *Rolling Stone*'s 2003 list of the 500 greatest albums of all time. Cale left the group after their second album, *White Light/White Heat* (1968). Reed's songwriting matured over the next few albums and, in 1971, he began a solo career. After his work with David Bowie produced his most successful album (in terms of sales), *Transformer* (1972), and his only hit, "Walk on the Wild Side," he recorded *Berlin* (1973), a rock opera about junkies and domestic abuse in the German city. *Metal Machine Music* (1975), his double album of amplifier feedback and noise, alienated most of his newfound fans, although Reed maintains it was a serious piece of work. "We reviewed that album in the magazine," says John Holmstrom, co-founder of *Punk* magazine. "We thought it was the best record ever made. To me it signaled the beginning of the punk era—it was kind of a nuclear bomb that wiped out everything before it."[1] In later years, Reed worked with a range of artists who included theater director Robert Wilson and painter/filmmaker Julian Schnabel. In 1996, the Velvet Underground was inducted into the Rock and Roll Hall of Fame. Reed married his longtime companion, performance artist Laurie Anderson, in April 2008.

NOTE

1. School of Visual Arts, "MFA Designer as Author: Guest Lectures, John Holmstrom." http://design.schoolofvisualarts.edu/weblog/guestlecture/.

Patti Smith (December 30, 1946–)

Patti Smith arose from the 1970s New York punk scene and influenced a generation of women who would grow up to be musicians, singers, and writers in the alternative music world. Unlike the singer/songwriters of the 1970s, Smith was a female singer for women who liked to rock. Just one look at her on the cover of her landmark 1975 album, *Horses*, wearing a man's shirt and tie, her hair all askew, immediately suggested that Smith was different. The Patti Smith Group was the first band from the CBGBs scene to put out an album, the first to attract mainstream media attention, and the first to reach listeners outside of New York. As a teenager in New Jersey, Smith took refuge in poetry, literature, and rock and roll. Inspired in part by French poet Arthur Rimbaud, American

Patti Smith in 1975. Smith was the first musician to move beyond the punk scene at CBGBs and the last musician to play there when it closed in 2006. (© Arista Records, Arista Records/Photofest)

beatnik writers, Rolling Stones guitarist Brian Jones, and the words of Bob Dylan, Smith would later fuse her love of language and loud guitars into her unique style of music. She moved to New York City in 1967, where she met and lived with art student and future photographer Robert Mapplethorpe while practicing her chosen craft at the time, painting. Over time, Smith shifted her focus from painting to writing. While dating playwright Sam Shepherd, the two writers coauthored and starred in the play *Cowboy Mouth*. She eventually began participating in a weekly poetry reading at St. Marks Church on the Lower East Side and invited Lenny Kaye, a rock writer and sometime guitarist, to accompany her while she read. In early 1974, when pianist Richard "DNV" Sohl started to play with them, they began to develop her signature style—a combination of musical and lyrical improvisation frequently based on the rhythm, chord changes, or lyrics of old rock and roll songs. In July 1975, the trio, aided by guitarist Tom Verlaine of Television, recorded Smith's original take on the song "Hey Joe," previously popularized by the Leaves and Jimi Hendrix. Mapplethorpe paid to have "Hey Joe" released on their own label, Mer Records, creating one of the first do-it-yourself "punk" singles. Smith was soon signed to Arista Records and, with guitarist Ivan Kral, drummer Jay Dee Daugherty, and producer John Cale, formerly of the Velvet Underground, they recorded Smith's groundbreaking debut, *Horses*. Released in November 1975, the album actually made it into the U.S. Top 50. While touring to support her second album, *Radio Ethiopia* (1976), Smith fell from a stage in Tampa, Florida, cracking two vertebrae in her neck. As she recuperated, she worked on a volume of poetry, *Babel*, and wrote and recorded *Easter*, featuring her hit single "Because the Night," written by Bruce Springsteen and reworked by Smith. After a final album, *Wave*, in 1979, Smith retired from rock and roll, moved to Detroit, and married former MC5 guitarist and leader of the Sonic Rendezvous Band, Fred Smith. For much of the 1980s, they raised their two children and lived a private life. Then, in 1988, she released *Dream of Life*, a comeback album cowritten and produced with Fred. After Fred's death from heart failure in 1994, Smith slowly made her way back into public life, recording a number of albums and performing and touring intermittently, often with her son, Jackson, on guitar. She moved back to New York City, where she remains a vital artistic force as she expresses herself through poetry, prose, photography, and music. In 2008, filmmaker Steven Sebring released a documentary about Smith entitled *Dream of Life*.

Winston Smith (born James Patrick Shannon Morey, May 27, 1952–)

A graphic designer and collage artist known to most people for his work with the San Francisco punk band the Dead Kennedys, Winston Smith appropriates images from the 1880s to the 1950s to create surreal collages that challenge societal or political norms. His work was first popularized by the Dead Kennedys when they used his artwork "Idol," which featured Jesus Christ nailed to a cross of dollars, as the cover for their 1981 EP *In God We Trust, Inc.* He also created the band's logo. After growing up in Oklahoma City, Smith spent almost seven years studying classical Renaissance art at the Academy of Fine Arts in Florence, Italy. He later won a scholarship to study cinema at the International University of Art in Florence and Rome. Smith then moved to San Francisco, where he worked as a roadie for San Francisco bands and began creating and distributing concert posters for bands he invented. As he said in 1998,

> There was a lot of art being done for bands in the initial punk scene that was godawful. I thought I could do a little better than some of the posters I saw. I wasn't involved in the scene in any deep sense and didn't really know anybody in any bands, so I kind of just made up posters for bands that didn't exist and clubs that didn't exist. I put them all over the city and people would collect them and even show up at the address of the club, which was a vacant lot somewhere.[1]

Smith was soon introduced to the Dead Kennedys' singer Jello Biafra and began collaborating with the band. Since then he has created album covers for Biafra, the Dead Kennedys, Green Day, the Burning Brides, and many others; worked as an illustrator for *Spin* magazine's Topspin political page; held a number of one-man shows of his artwork; and released several books of his art: *Act Like Nothing's Wrong* (1994), *Art Crime* (1999), and *All Riot on the Western Front* (2004). Smith married Chick Fontaine, a San Francisco poster artist, in 2006.

NOTE

1. Sinker, Daniel, ed. *We Owe You Nothing* (New York: Akashic Books, 2001), 156.

Penelope Spheeris (December 2, 1945–)

A filmmaker noted in punk circles primarily for her first feature-length film, the 1981 documentary *The Decline of Western Civilization, Part 1,* which exposed the Los Angeles punk scene to the rest of the world, Penelope Spheeris continued her look at punks in *Suburbia*, a 1984 film she wrote and directed. Although not a documentary, *Suburbia* was widely praised for its gritty realism and sobering look at the lives of these ignored and often abused young people. As a young woman, Spheeris worked as a waitress to put herself through film school and eventually graduated with a Master of Fine Arts in theater arts from UCLA. Initially she was a film editor and a cinematographer before forming her own company in 1974, Rock 'n' Reel, the first Los Angeles production company specializing in music videos. In the late 1970s, she produced short films for Albert Brooks, eventually producing his feature film *Real Life*. In the 1970s and 1980s she produced, directed, and edited videos for major rock bands, and in 1992 she directed her first film for a major studio, *Wayne's World*. With the success of that venture, she was asked to direct *The Beverly Hillbillies* (1993), *The Little Rascals* (1994), *Black Sheep* (1996), *Senseless* (1998), and others. She also worked as a writer for the television series *Roseanne*. Despite her other projects, Spheeris returns to music every few years. She continued her *Decline of Western Civilization* franchise with Part II (the Metal Years) in 1988 and Part III, focusing on young punks in the late 1990s, in 1997.

Mike Watt (December 20, 1957–)

The bassist for the Minutemen, fIREHOSE, and the reunited Stooges, Mike Watt pioneered the art of touring econo style: booking his own tours, traveling by van, loading his own equipment, selling inexpensive T-shirts, and playing in a three-piece band. Watt was born in Virginia, but his family moved to San Pedro, California, when he was ten. There he met friend and future bandmate Dennes Boon (D. Boon). Together Watt and Boon caught the initial wave of punk, listening first to the Ramones and Television, then the Germs and the Dils. They formed their first band in 1978 with drummer George Hurley and created the Minutemen a year later. Watt explained,

> The "minute" meant more like [the adjective] minute. Like we were small compared to a big arena rock band. And the other reason for the name—I had a bunch of names on a paper, and D. Boon picked that

one. He liked it because there was some right-wing group who used the name. We thought, we'll call ourselves the same thing—there goes their power! It'll dilute it and confuse things.[1]

Many of the Minutemen's early songs were shorter than a minute, although they stretched it out to almost three on their later recordings. The band released five albums before Boon died in a car crash in 1985. The following year, guitarist Ed Crawford convinced Watt to start playing again, and they formed fIREHOSE, which recorded and toured until the early 1990s. In 1995, Watt released his first solo record, *Ball-Hog or Tugboat?*, with guest appearances by members of Nirvana, Beastie Boys, Soul Asylum, Sonic Youth, and Screaming Trees. Since then he has recorded as a solo artist, performed with Kira Roessler (formerly of Black Flag) in dos, their two-bass-only band, and worked as a sideman with other bands—most notably with Iggy Pop when the Stooges reunited in 2003. A film about the Minutemen, *We Jam Econo*, was released in 2006. By 2008, Watt estimated he had been on sixty-six tours.

NOTE

1. Mike Watt's Hoot Page, "Watt Bio." http://hootpage.com/hoot_wattbio.html.

Butch Vig (Born Bryan David Vigorson, August 2, 1957–)

Credited with creating the "grunge" sound—or at least with first capturing it on record—when he produced Nirvana's breakthrough album, *Nevermind*, Butch Vig became a sought-after producer with the success of that album. Raised in Wisconsin, Vig was in college at the University of Wisconsin at Madison when he formed his first band, Spooner. In 1979, Vig and Steve Marker (also in Spooner) created a small studio with a four-track recording machine in Marker's basement and later created their own label, Boat Records, to release records by Spooner and other bands they liked. While producing Spooner and a side project, Fire Town, in 1988, Vig began to gain a reputation as a producer as young bands traveled to Madison to record with him. He recorded Nirvana for Seattle's Sub Pop label in 1989, and when the band signed to Geffen Records they insisted that Vig record their first major-label release. The result was *Nevermind*. Even as he continued to produce punk and alternative bands, including L7, Sonic Youth, Smashing Pumpkins, and Soul Asylum, Vig reunited with his friends from Spooner, brought Scottish singer Shirley Manson on board, and created the band Garbage. Their self-titled debut was released in 1995 to critical acclaim and strong sales, and the band was nominated for a Grammy award for best new artist. While Garbage has recorded and released new material every few years—*Version 2.0* (1998), *Beautiful Garbage* (2001), *Bleed Like Me* (2005), and a greatest hits package *Absolute Garbage* (2007)—Vig continues his production work with musicians ranging from Jimmy Eat World to the Subways to Green Day.

Tim Yohannan (August 15, 1945–April 3, 1998)

Tim Yohannan began the underground radio show Maximum Rocknroll (MRR) on KPFA in Berkeley, California, in the late 1970s. In the early 1980s, Yohannan turned MRR into a reasonably professional magazine and built it into the first punk zine of any consequence to see nationwide distribution. As punk scene reports began filtering in to Berkeley from around the world, the MRR radio show was syndicated across America and Europe and the zine brought underground bands to international attention. According to writer Gavin McNett, "The MRR explosion was the first truly global, grassroots youth phenomenon in history, and it did for some of us what the Web would later do for the culture at large: it removed the limitations of place and substituted for them an unplumbable pool of information and discourse."[1] A product of the 1960s counterculture, Yohannan saw that MRR accepted no corporate ads, and he donated its profits to charity even while continuing to work a blue-collar job at the Lawrence Hall of Science at the University of California, Berkeley. His house served as MRR headquarters. Renowned for his staunch DIY philosophy and stringent ideology, he helped establish the Blacklist Mailorder service, the Epicenter Zone record store and community center, and the Gilman Street Project, an all-ages, nonprofit, collectively organized music and performance venue in Berkeley. Tim Chandler of Mutant Pop Records, an Oregon-based independent label, called Yohannan "undeniably one of the most important figures in the history of American punk rock."[2] Yohannan passed away in 1998 after battling lymphoma for several years.

NOTES

1. McNett, Gavin. "The Day Punk Died," *Salon*, http://archive.salon.com/music/feature/1998/04/17feature.html.
2. *Rolling Stone*. "Punk Publisher Tim Yohannan Dead at 52," www.rollingstone.com/artists/nofx/articles/story/5926602/punk_publisher_tim_yohannan_dead_at_52.

Primary Documents from the Punk Subculture

1. Ian MacKaye Interview

Musician (Minor Threat, Fugazi), cofounder of Dischord Records

Ian MacKaye has remained closely connected to the Washington, D.C., punk scene for almost thirty years. In that time, he's formed a lot of opinions and conclusions about punk rock, its impact, and its place in society and, as a result, he is frequently consulted by many, if not most, documentary film makers and writers working on punk-related projects. Like Jello Biafra, Henry Rollins, and other punks who have been active since the early 1980s, MacKaye has earned his share of critics who disagree with his lifestyle or politics. But he remains committed to the promise of early punk and its DIY and anticorporate principles. With his band Fugazi (active from 1987 to 2002), MacKaye took an all-encompassing DIY approach to business. They had no outside management and handled all the logistics of touring, recording, and press relations themselves. They famously played all-ages shows in unconventional venues with admission prices as low as $5, often to benefit worthy social causes. With Jeff Nelson, cofounder of Dischord Records, MacKaye has worked to build a reputation for upright business practices; they have never had a contract with any of their bands, preferring to base *their agreements on trust. While many of the great independent labels spawned by punk have disappeared, Dischord Records carries on. This interview took place on May 15, 2009.*

What does the word "punk" mean to you personally?

The definition of "punk," like many words, is really very personal, or it's multi-layered, I should say. My entrance to punk was in late '78 when my friends in high school were talking about new wave/punk and listening to David Bowie and Iggy Pop and the Ramones. There was this weird other music that wasn't on the radio. My initial reaction was one of derision. I thought it was ridiculous—"Why would you listen to this stuff when you have this great rock and roll?" But most of that was because I was intimidated by it because it was an area that I knew nothing about and it felt dark in a way. It was something that was not in the light. But when I first started listening to it, it took me a while to understand it because I had been so conditioned by radio to hear what music should sound like. To hear music being created and delivered in a different fashion was hard on the ears. I've often used the metaphor that it is like being raised on hamburgers and French fries and then going to a Vietnamese restaurant. When you sit down you don't recognize what's in front of you but you know it's dinner. It's a meal and it's probably better for you. Once I started to understand the music, it revealed to me this vast underground world, this counterculture that has always existed and exists and will always exist. The question is, "How do you punch through the wall that separates mainstream from counterculture?" You need to access portals, and to me punk rock was a portal. That's why I shy away from ever specifically saying what punk rock is. I just say it's a free space. It's also a moniker. It's a term that I use, but someone else might use the word jazz. If you think about the word jazz, you could mean jazz music, but what's it mean now? Who knows? It's wide open and it's one of the beauties of language in a way. As specific as a term can be, you have to connect with people to agree on terminology before you can even get to what the specifics are. As passionate as I might be about the free space, there are other people who would say, "He's full of s***. Punk is a particular chord structure, or a rebellious attitude." I was never a nihilist or interested in vandalism. I'm not a thief. I don't believe in destruction, yet I'm still a punk. So how can punk be a nihilistic, destructive thing?

So what makes you say you're a punk? Because you like the music, or is there something deeper, an attitude toward life?

I think it's a term that is up for grabs. For me it was a portal to the counterculture, and that's where I feel I belong. My life makes sense to me when I'm in an environment where people are challenging conventional thinking. Conventional thinking is what puts countries into ridiculous military and criminal operations in other lands. People just not challenging these things, not thinking, they're just following. I wanted to be in an environment where people weren't just rejecting everything; they were investigating things before they accepted them. They took an inventory. When I got into punk rock, it revealed to me that there was a part of society that didn't necessarily think music should sound a certain way, didn't think that you should dress a certain way. Sexuality was wide open, philosophy was wide open, and theology was wide open. People who really challenged the idea that there should be a straight, single path in society. Punk rock was my portal, so I feel I must be a punk. It doesn't mean anything ultimately. It just doesn't mean a damn thing. But what does the word "America" mean? It doesn't mean anything. It's just an agreed-upon term. At least with punk, it's self-definition. I recognize my life as part of a world that actually wants to engage with what is being presented and decide whether or not it makes sense.

The two streams of thought I hear about punk relate to questioning authority and the do-it-yourself approach to life, although I think they're both related. At times there has been violence related to the questioning of authority, but most of the time there was not. There was a period (1980s) when there was more violence than today.

And that period was a birthing, and birthing is attended by friction. And that violence was a manifest of that friction, and it was quite often not the punks who were chafing, frankly. In my early days of punk, I remember I cut my hair and I got yelled at by jocks. The moment I made this decision that I wanted to be part of something different and have an outward manifestation of that decision, I cut my hair off, wore weird clothes, went to the thrift store and bought clothes, found an old leather jacket. Those decisions to look different resulted in harassment and ultimately violence. Especially when you live in Washington [D.C.] and are close to a lot of military bases. There were a lot of military dudes coming in who were primed to wreck "the other." At some point we decided we would fight back. I was a pacifist as a kid, totally antiwar, nonviolent. But by the time I was into punk rock, we decided we had to put a stop to this and fight back. Also, I had been well-trained in the D.C. public school system. I was accustomed to being attacked. But violence can ultimately only produce more violence. It doesn't have any effect otherwise. So there may have been some rational violence that gave way to unreasonable irrational violence. I'm not saying one's any better than the other, I'm merely saying that in my mind I had a conceit that there was some purpose or reason for it. I actually had a philosophy that I would bruise the ego and not the body and I never sent people to hospitals. But there were definitely people going to the hospital.

It all had to do with the friction of something new being created. Also, the media only picked up on the nihilist and sensationalist and absurdist aspect of punk rock. If you look at network television's portrayal of punk rock, the *Quincy* show and *CHiPS*, punks are always completely violent lunatics. This resonated with people who thought that's how punk is supposed to be. So we found ourselves then visited by new legions of punks who came to punk through these weird depictions. So they were not only violent, because that's what they thought they were supposed to do, but they were embarrassing because we saw it as a ridiculous portrayal. So that's a good example of what the media can do in terms of putting a cancer into something that was ultimately an artistic, creative, thinking community. Books of punk rock often talk about the fighting, or this guy overdosed, or someone was throwing bags of vomit, and all of these disgusting things. People talk about all of this idiocy, but no one seems to understand that, yes, those things did occur yet there were so many people who felt passionate about it because they were building something, the music, the community, and the freedom and the liberation and the identity they felt in a world that frowns on collective identity outside of the mainstream. The real story was not the sensationalist stuff but that people felt so passionate about something that was really important to them. I think it was the first time in American history that kids, teenagers, formed their own bands, wrote their own songs, put on their own shows, put out their own records, put out their own fanzines, created their own touring network, all under the radar of the organized music industry. Profit was not a driving motive; there was no profit to be made, yet people spent all day living this. It was a real organic network.

Why do you think it happened at that time?

I suspect a couple of things lined up. For those of us born in the early '60s, we were aware of or part of the social revolution that came along with the hippies. The antiwar movement, the civil rights movement. There was a reason, you knew you were supposed to be doing something. And if you lived through Watergate, you knew the government couldn't always be trusted, that power corrupts. It's always been true and always will be true. By the '70s though, there seemed to be this white noise. In my high school, the only form of rebellion came in the form of self-destruction, getting high or drinking. There were people propelling themselves toward college and jobs—not bad people, they were just following that road. And then you had this stoner crowd and that was the rebellion. Those choices were not enough for me. There wasn't a choice that said, "We reject the American way, we question authority, we don't trust the government, we know that there are wrongs that we want to right." In the late '70s there was a real dearth of those qualities. And I think the music industry, the rock industry, had become so removed from anything real, that there was this gap where people could step in. There was a fallow field. I think that at that time, there was Peter Frampton and Led Zeppelin and all those people, and the way music was being recorded and the mass media was being presented, it had just become unmoored. It was like they were floating so far above earth that they gave other people room. It wasn't just an opportunity, it was a necessity. If we wanted to see music, we just had to do it.

What do you think about the number of bands that started on small labels and now, like Green Day and others, they've moved to major labels?

I'm not critical of them at all. The only thing I will say is that they're not punk bands. There may be punks in the band, but there's no such thing as a punk band on a major label. That's just antithetical. It doesn't make any sense. It doesn't mean that they're bad bands or that their music isn't any good. I honestly don't know because I don't listen to their music. When I got into punk rock, I turned the radio off forever. I just don't listen to major-label music. I realized that I had tapped into a world of music that was really interesting, and I realized that the world has been producing music every second of every day, and since electricity and recording devices, it's been documented. There's far more music than I could ever listen to in my lifetime. So why would I spend a lot of time listening to music that's been carefully processed to drill a hole in my ear and manipulate me? I'm just not interested in that.

Many independent labels have come and gone over the years. How has Dischord managed to stay in business?

In American society, if you do something that's successful, there's this idea that you should now embrace the way successful people do things. So suddenly, for example, you would bring in management, because that's what successful people do. But you're already successful. Why would you consider changing anything you do? I didn't ever believe in changing. I didn't understand why we would have to change. When Fugazi first started playing, people would say, "Well, you can do benefits now, but at some point you're going to have stop doing them." Or, "You can charge $5 now, but at some point you're going to have to charge more." Or, "You can book your own shows now, but at some point you're going to have to get some help." But why? What's the reason? It's because people assume you get to a certain level and then you have to embrace the structure of the existing industry. And the only reason people think that is because no one ever did it another way.

Punk's been around for thirty years now. Where do things seem to be heading? What does punk mean in 2009?

I don't look into the future, and I've never been a futurist. Punk will never die. It existed much longer than thirty years, it was just called something different. I think that folk was punk, rockabilly was punk, rock was punk, blues was punk, hip-hop was punk. It's all basically the same thing—it's all basically the free space, and the free space can never die. So the future always looks bright, because there's always a new crop of human beings. It might be kids coming up or people coming out. There are people who grow up in our world caught in the machinations of our society and then one day they come out of it—"You know what, I reject that"—and they find themselves engaging in a practice or a community where people are liberating themselves. You usually find it with kids, because they don't even know they have to be folded into the batter. It's not usually until your late teens or twenties that you start to think, "I guess I have to do it this way." Kids will say, "What do you mean? I don't want to do that."

Just as I can't imagine arriving somewhere and having someone say, "Here's the clothes you're going to wear," I can't imagine someone hearing, "Here's your rebellion, and here's the music you'll play." There will always be someone who will say, "You don't tell me how to rebel. You don't tell me how to express myself." It's an organic process, and that's forever. It's never going to go away.

People ask me all the time if there's something going on today, and I say, just like in 1981, it's underground. It will always be underground—that's why it's called "the underground." It will always be off the radar of the mainstream. And even for those of us who aren't exactly in the mainstream, you have to be in the basements. Those kids will never stop creating. There will be times where there are creative bubbles that have more of an effect. Obviously the early American punk scene had a tremendous cultural effect on this country. Much more than most people realize.

2. Jeff Nelson Interview

Musician (Teen Idles, Minor Threat), cofounder of Dischord Records

In 1980, while drumming for the hardcore band the Teen Idles, Jeff Nelson and his friend Ian MacKaye founded Dischord Records in Washington, D.C. Even before releasing their first record, they left the Teen Idles and created the infamous hardcore band Minor Threat. Since Minor Threat's break-up in 1983, Nelson has played in a number of bands, including Egg Hunt and Skewbald/Grand Union (both with MacKaye) and Feedbag, Wonderama, and High-Back Chairs. In 2003, he moved to the historic "Old West End" of Toledo, Ohio, where, in addition to his work with Dischord, he works as a political activist and plays with the band Fast Piece of Furniture. The band released their first album in 2007 on Nelson's label, Adult Swim Records. After twenty-eight years, Nelson and MacKaye still run Dischord, making it one of the longest-lived independent labels. This interview took place on December 2, 2008. As the history of Nelson's band Minor Threat has been covered extensively and well (most notably in Michael Azerrad's book Our Band Could Be Your Life*), this interview focused on what initially attracted him to punk and his current view of punk culture.*

When you started the Teen Idles, did you self-identify as a punk?

Well, it took me a while to get into the punk culture. At the time there were two very distinct camps—there was new wave, and there was punk. And I very much identified with new wave before punk. I heard the Sex Pistols record, *Talking Heads '77*, and Bob Marley all on the same night. I liked the Bob Marley and the Talking Heads right away, but with the Sex Pistols it took another three or four months before I realized that it was amazing. I think everybody basically came to the punk scene in their own distinct route and through their own combinations of friends—not peer pressure necessarily—or stuff they heard on the radio or things they read about.

So I think it's different for each person and the length of time they were a punk or dressed like a punk is different for each person. I was a geek and loved the Beatles and liked rock and had discovered pot and beer and was very taken with the underground and the small scale of the bands and the shows and records. You had to seek them out. It was fun to feel like you were one of the few who realized how great this stuff was and to belong then to a group of people who were equally interested in new and edgier music that was less glossy and packaged and commercialized. And increasingly more aggressive.

I would say the transition from new wave to punk happened because you wanted something more aggressive and from punk to hardcore because you thought it could still be more aggressive. For me dressing punk was a way to get attention, though there is a huge disagreement between people about this. Some people would argue that punk is an attitude and once you're punk, you're punk the rest of your life. It's a way of living and it's an attitude. I can see what they're talking about, but I think for plenty of people, the majority of people in the punk scenes around the world, it's just a stage they're going through. Some people think that's a horrible thing to say, because it sounds dismissive. But for a certain number of years I wanted to dress shockingly and to look threatening and fierce. But after a certain number of years I decided I didn't like scaring people and didn't want to make old people nervous. As much as I thought old German stuff was great looking, I didn't want to be thought of as a Nazi.

So for me, the dress part of it was a way to stand out, to be different, and to belong to a new, smaller group. It was like a clique, a group that you feel you belong to. It was a way to stand out and be part of a group and, I guess, either get attention or gain stature by dressing a certain way. Either people think you're cool or people decide not to beat you up because they're not sure what to think about you. It was a way to gain grudging acceptance from some of the tougher elements in high school.

It's always amazing to hear stories of punks getting beat up for the way they looked when you look at pictures of them in the early 1980s and most don't look that different or shocking.

One of the greatest things that has been lost with the passage of time is context. The Sex Pistols record is not that shocking when you listen to it now. It was very shocking back them.

We're often asked, "What do you think about punk now?" I first say I really don't know much about punk now. It's still going on, much to my amazement. I really can't believe it's still going on. I don't begrudge the kids now, loving the bands that they love. The current bands with kids their age, to them it's fresh. All that being said, it's hard for me to look at it and see. Every kid in the world has a tattoo now, it seems. Tattoos were incredibly rare in the scene when we grew up. It was what sailors and gang members and people in jail had. Everyone is pierced and tattooed now—to me it's hilarious that the punk look is still thought of as threatening, because to me it's so safe now. But then I realize that there's probably still no shortage of jocks at plenty of suburban and rural high schools willing to beat up a scrawny kid who looks a little bit different. It might seem like a safe thing to look like a punk now from my perspective, but from the perspective of a kid who's just doing it, I suppose there's no shortage of people being shocked or that they get a rise out of.

It's just rebellion. I'm sure for many, many, many kids it's rebellion against their parents and against their families.

Did you find that as the number of bands grew in Washington that there was a sense of camaraderie, or was the scene more competitive?

There was mostly camaraderie. People were proud to say where they were from, Bethesda or Bailey's Crossroad or D.C., but most were proud to be from the D.C. area. The only thing that changed that later for a lot of bands was the interminable question, "Are you guys straight edge?" They just got so sick of having the large shadow of straight edge and Minor Threat over them, which is what people thought of when they thought of D.C. I think a lot of bands got sick of that. Some knew Ian, and knew he was a regular guy, and they would just answer the questions and finish the interview, but others really came to resent it. The whole straight edge thing just really did, for them, represent the opposite of fun. Some took it to the extreme with bent edge.

I think Dischord was very unifying for the scene. Not every band was on Dischord, but most of the bands that made a mark were, with the exception of the Bad Brains. So in that sense it was very unifying for the scene. But you can't put out every band's record.

So there was a sense of camaraderie when you saw another punk on the street, but there were so few of us that you would sort of salute each other.

Many of the labels like Dischord and SST that sprung up around 1980 were founded by bands that wanted to put out their own records and couldn't get someone else to do it. Why was that possible at that time? I'm sure there were bands in the late 1960s that also wanted to put their music out, but they didn't start labels.

I'm guessing that everything we did had been done before in the 1960s with garage punk bands. I might be wrong, but it would be a modern conceit to think we were the first to have our own fanzines or put out our own 7 inches. In the 1950s you could go and record an acetate in the little recording booths, sort of like a photo booth. You could play them like twenty times before they started to degrade. And there were all these tiny little labels putting out blues and jazz and "race music." So I think other genres had their own versions of the same thing.

Certainly the advent of the Xerox machine was very helpful in making flyers. Seriously, you cannot do the same things with a mimeograph machine. So we benefited greatly from that and other earlier incarnations of do-it-yourselfers would not have had that. I do think we deserve credit for having the gumption and doing it ourselves. We had no idea that we'd still be doing it twenty-some years later.

Many labels have come and gone over the years. How is it that Dischord is still in business after all this time?

Ian and I talked about this all the time. And I think he's correct in saying the slow pace at which we put out records compared to SST and Sub Pop has helped. Some companies put out so many records so quickly and expanded so fast and expanded their range of music so fast. Some of them grew and became huge and successful, but others just caved in under the weight of their unwieldy catalog and lost their original fanbase. We've stayed a pretty darn small operation and have ridiculously economic budgets for everything from the studio to artwork.

We never overextended ourselves with lavish studio budgets or tour support. There were a lot of things I wish we could do and would love to do for the bands to make it easier for them to tour because in the end I think it would behoove [sic] everybody. But by not overextending ourselves, we put out the records and give the bands a leg up. Over the years, the name Dischord came to mean something. To this day, we put out a record then the rest of it is pretty much up to the band. They have to tour and make good on their record. If the record is great, then word of mouth is the best promotion. But touring helps a lot and actively continuing to be a good band helps.

We've been very lucky to work with a lot of great bands. And anything Ian is involved in gets a lot of attention, so I think it helps that he's half the label. We've always tried to sell our records at a reasonable price and give people a [good] value for their dollar. We put out stuff that we think is good and try to do it in a very standup way, and I think in the end, the people have respect for us and we have street credibility.

There's a lot of talk in punk about what's punk and what isn't. If someone sells a lot of records, can they still be punk?

Good Charlotte is a great example of this. I don't own any of their records and haven't heard anything they've done recently, but I thought some of their early stuff was pretty catchy. I don't think less of them because they have made it. The same with Green Day, they're probably the best example. I don't have any of their records, either. They've had all the cries of sellout, but that album they did, *American Idiot*, has some pretty great songs that are thematically spot-on with taking Bush and the neo-cons to task. They do it masterfully. I would still describe that as punk music, and I think most of their fans would describe themselves as punk.

Modern music to me is so weird. I don't listen to much music and therefore much new music. With the advent of downloads, the major labels are not nearly the powerhouses that they were in the 1970s, when they would nurture an artist and stick with them through a few albums. They could push certain supergroups really effectively.

Within the punk scene, major labels are not playing as much of a role as they were for quite a few years after Nirvana. Back then they came in and were huge, annoying, frustrating competition for the already-established smaller labels. I haven't heard this conversation much these days, but there was always much derision of major labels. The idea that if something is on a major label, it can't be any good. It's so dumb because everything we grew up on—The Beatles, Led Zeppelin, Black Sabbath, Deep Purple—that's just a few, they were all on major labels. So major labels can do great good and bring out very good stuff. You just need good people at the labels and good artists and good timing. I would agree that the best aspects of punk are realized when it's the do-it-yourself model. I think that's the purest form of punk, when it's from the heart, from your bedroom, from your garage. For the same reasons that a band's first record is often their best record—Minor Threat, Dead Kennedys—usually the first one is the purest. With punk stuff it's usually youth and anger and excitement and enthusiasm and naïveté all combined to create something that's homegrown. I don't think that's exclusive to punk, but it's certainly what punk has always been all about. I do think that punk can still exist on a larger scale and can be commercially viable, but it starts to become a different creature.

In this new book, *Radio Silence* (by Nathan Nedorostek and Anthony Pappalardo), we have quite a description of life precomputer. How did one put together a flyer? What did found art consist of back then, and how was it both more limiting and better than [using] the computer? So there's a discussion in there about that. How do you book a show, how do you hear about a band, how do you get your music out there? It's completely different from now. How incredibly everything changed—if you're just a band or a kid who's written his own music, you can put it together in your bedroom and then burn CDs or put it on your Web site. In an hour you can be broadcasting it around the world. It's incredibly liberating, but also I think the hurdles that used to be in place helped to sort stuff out—you had to be pretty serious and pretty driven. There were still plenty of crappy vinyl records that were put out, but there's just so much more crap to wade through now. As much as it's easier to get your stuff out there now, you're out there with thousands and thousands of others doing the exact same thing. In the early punk scene, it was very much word of mouth, trying to find clubs in other cities and writing to them. It was much more primitive and an awful lot of work but much more welcoming than now. I think it's probably much more impersonal now.

3. Jello Biafra Interview (Excerpt)
   Punk Planet 18, May/June 1997

Musician, political activist, spoken-word artist, founder of Alternative Tentacles record label

For more than thirty years, Jello Biafra has savored his role as a truth-teller in the punk community. Daniel Sinker and Joel Schalit of Punk Planet *have called his band, the Dead Kennedys, "arguably the most ideologically important band in the history of American punk politics" and credit them with "injecting real leftist politics into American punk culture." In the early 1980s, Biafra pushed people to think for themselves and to question everything as he worked to open up the hardcore scene by releasing other bands' music on the Dead Kennedy's record label, Alternative Tentacles. As a result of this work and a heavily publicized obscenity trial, Biafra became the most well-known "star" in the hardcore scene. But the celebrity he earned caused problems. He was branded a sell-out by some punks, including Tim Yohannan, editor of the influential zine* Maximum Rocknroll, *which refused to accept advertisements for records released by Alternative Tentacles. In 1994, Biafra suffered head and leg injuries after being attacked and taunted as a "rich rock star" by a group of punks at the Gilman Street Project in Berkeley. When this interview took place in 1997, Biafra was still ostracized by some in the punk community for the crime of not being "punk" enough.*

So where do you think we are at this point in the culture wars?

As much as commercial music has gotten dumbed down, just like in the '70s before punk happened, I think overall the '90s is the best time to be around for music. In particular because now you have a choice: if you are not into the crap that's fed to you by major labels and MTV, you can find any kind of music you like, and it's back in print again. In the '70s it was impossible to get any rockabilly records, for instance. Now, if you like rockabilly, you can pick up stuff by the '50s originals or go see a band in your hometown that sounds exactly like them. [laughs] The same goes for early punk or early hardcore—you can get the real stuff or see their imitators and hope they have some inkling of the heart and soul of the original. And that goes for jazz or just about anything. Contemporary music? I try to pay as little attention to it as possible. Whenever my girlfriend has the so-called "alternative" station on in her car, it drives me nuts. On the surface it sounds like what they are shoving at us now are bad imitations of Pearl Jam and Nirvana, but when you listen a little closer (especially to the commercial pop punk bands), I find no difference between them and the most horrible era of the Eagles. The only difference is that the guitars are louder. In Britain, there are people doing blatant imitations of Hüsker Dü, although they don't write songs nearly as well. If I want to hear Hüsker Dü, I'll just put on a Hüsker Dü record. We have that choice. Besides, being unoriginal is not punk.

What are the political implications of all this? Do you think the fact that bands like Rancid or the Offspring (that were at least perceived as having a radical agenda) sold millions of records has had an effect on mass consciousness?

All those bands got to where they are in part because they are good at what they do—not even the most vehement backstabber can deny that. And if they have a political impact, it will be greater if they take the bull by the horns and come out more in support of political organizing and organizations in such ways that I have already suggested. Green Day did a high-profile benefit for Food Not Bombs, who are so controversial even in the radical world that I know of no other large rock band that ever went to bat for them. They raised $50,000. I don't think a small underground show would have benefitted Food Not Bombs as much. They would raise $400 or $500 bucks and everybody would feel good in the end, but Food Not

Bombs could spend that money in half a day trying to feed homeless people. I will be curious to see if there is a long-term ripple effect or not, because people who work in record stores tell me that some of the mall kids who got into punk through Bad Religion or the other bands you mention, six months later look into the roots and pick up a Dead Kennedys record. They then find that the lyrics have a little different vibe and attitude connected to them. I'm frustrated about how many new people are going to discover Dead Kennedys through this scene and have no clue as to where we were at and can't understand why I don't want to re-form the band and do a Sex Pistols' Filthy Lucre Tour. They don't understand what punk was or what it is still supposed to be. Not only that, they refuse to understand. But I'm really hoping it will ripple down to people taking a long hard look at clouding their future with what their parents, teachers, and the mass media tell them to do. The ripple effect has happened to some degree already. It doesn't mean so much to me when people come up to me and say, "Jello! Dead Kennedys rule! You're God! Blah! Blah! Could you please give me an iron-on tattoo for my nuts!" That doesn't mean too much. What does is when somebody says, "I listened to your music and listened to your words and decided to quit majoring in business and do something else with my life." And then sometimes they'll hand me a record or a magazine or a video they have done. In another case, somebody I knew in childhood went the fast track to a cushy job as a professor at the University of Colorado, and then got so disgusted by being thrust into a room of three hundred frat boys and rich kids, that he quit the job—where he had guaranteed tenure—and went off to teach history in a rural middle school where he could actually help kids learn. He said a lot of people in his class don't speak English very well and some are so discouraged that they have never written a paper in their life, so he grades according to effort. People who don't show up for other classes show up for his and even try to write something; I think that's really important. So that's an example of what I think is the heart and soul of punk, just as I think it was the heart and soul of hippies when they were radical, the beats, and many others throughout history.

Many punks seem to assume that radical culture can replace radical political practice.

It can't. Culture can help initiate better politics, while politics can be used to suppress culture—they go hand in hand. Look at the investigation into Death Row Records. They would like nothing more than to pin some kind of criminal indictment on Dr. Dre, so they can discredit every word that every Death Row artist ever said. I think the only reason why major labels picked up on grunge and punk to begin with was to avoid a whole generation of suburban white kids getting their political knowledge from angry black rappers. They don't want white kids to know that things are that bad for a large number of people. They would much rather have people with shoe-gazer lyrics: "Oh, boo-hoo, my girlfriend left me, I'm so depressed. I'm white, middle-class, and confused. Gee, I feel so sorry for myself." That's the major-label lyrical angle.

But going back to my point. So much of the punk community seems to think that cultural activity is a replacement for political practice.

I would counter that there is no punk community among that group of people. It's a safe little punk womb to have *Maximum Rocknroll* as your bible and to think the world's most important issue is whether Jawbreaker sold out, while ignoring the homeless people outside. That's not community. Bickering endlessly over stuff that doesn't matter is not community, it's junior high.

So you think there is no cohesive social group that can be referred to as the "punk community"?

There are threads of it, but punk has gotten so popular that the name gets attached to all sorts of things—everything from Jawbreaker to Brutal Truth. There are all kinds of communities there, all networking with each other. None is as tight culturally as the death metal [an intense, fast sub-genre of heavy metal with extremely distorted guitars and vocalists who use a low-pitched guttural growl to "sing" dark and/or apocalyptic lyrics] community, where you have people in Norway swapping tapes with people in Malaysia, and all the bands sound more than a little bit alike. And isn't it ironic that death metal is the first form of rock music that has caught on with poor people all over the world? When I was in Brazil I was told that all rock music and punk was scorned by the people of the slums. It didn't speak to them, they thought of it as a bourgeois art form they didn't want to have anything to do with. They would rather listen to samba or death metal. Death metal is popular from Moldavia to Cuba.

Going back to this question of punk politics, it seems to me that radical punks have a lot of problems forming alliances with each other. It seems that Tim Yohannan [founder of the *Maximum Rocknroll* fanzine] has reproduced the worst aspects of the old left in his empire.

If not the old right! He reminds me a lot of Joe McCarthy these days and Ben Weasel reminds me of Lee Atwater. I got a whiff of all that as a kid and I'm very grateful that my parents were open enough to explain to me what was going on and have me watch the news and educate me about it.

Maximum Rocknroll seems dead set on this line of sectarian purity, where anything that creates a basis for mass support is looked on with suspicion and ultimately rejected as a sellout.

It's the same kind of fundamentalist mindset that makes fundamentalist Christians so dangerous, and the same mindset that has isolated the animal rights and vegan movements. You take one step out of line and they bite your head off. Young people who are curious about the politics spend ten minutes with people like that and they decide they would rather be apathetic. This is what has turned a lot of people off to punk politics.

So what are the solutions? Where do we go from here?

The underground scene is still a cool way to meet a lot of cool people, see a lot of interesting bands, and get a lot of food for thought, but people have to remain curious and get their brain-activity food from other places besides punk. Many of my spoken-word shows are at universities, and the people who bring me in are either political activists, who may listen to Tracy Chapman or the Cocteau Twins, or something like that. In fact, there was a whole tour where people kept saying, "I'm really getting into alternative rock now. Do you like the Cocteau Twins?" It happened again and again, and to this day I've never heard them! But what I'm saying is that I discovered that a lot of vibrant-minded activists either had nothing to do with punk by default or actively despised punk because their opinion of it had been tainted by fundamentalists and crusties. The other people who brought me in were conservatives, who just happened to be on the student activities committee, and since my fee was lower than other people's they figured they would get their money's worth! So it's a fascinating spectrum of people to talk to and absorb ideas from.

Writing the name of a British band that broke up fifteen years ago on the back of the jacket you bought at the mall does not make you radical, it doesn't even make you intelligent. In some cases it makes other people laugh and ask whether they have heard a single note of the Abrasive Wheels before you reproduced their album cover on the back of the jacket you bought the day before. I think being radical means interacting more with a lot of different kinds of people and making up your own mind about where you fit in and what you want to do. I didn't agree with the hard line that Crass or MDC took over the years, but it helped me decide what line I wanted to take instead. Namely, live my life the way I wanted to, but not to the point where it made me a miserable, dangerous person. You have to identify what you as an individual can do: What are your skills? How do they fit in? Are you somebody who is making a lot of money at a lawyer or computer job but doesn't have a lot of free time?

Well, funneling money to organizations that need it is one good place to start. Phil Ochs ridiculed that in his original version of "Love Me, I'm a Liberal," but it's far better than spending your money on Wall Street, rare coins, or old colored-vinyl punk collectibles. Or if you have a lot of free time, there are a lot of people with activist skills who need help, be it clinic defense, environmental work, or grassroots political campaigns to get somebody with a heart elected to a city council or a school board or even the mayor's office, depending on the town. Richard Hunter, who used to play bass for Killbilly and is now in I, the Jury, just ran for mayor of Fort Worth, Texas, because he gave a s***. What really terrified the powers that be was that he was running second in the polls up until election day, when a family-values guy, who had gone the stealth-candidate route through right-wing churches, came in ahead of him, as did a black activist. But he made a lot of noise and inspired a lot of respect, and hopefully he inspired a lot of people to try the same thing.

I'm down with both radical resistance and trying to do what can be done through the system. That is one of the reasons I ran for mayor way back when. And all this should have an end in mind. Corporate dictatorship is heading for a train wreck, and that train wreck will happen in our lifetime. They are throwing so many people out of work in this country that the people they depend on to buy their products won't have money to buy them anymore, and a lot of them are already hopping mad. They may be falling for Rush Limbaugh and the militia movement in the short run, but in the long run when the s*** goes down I hope it doesn't become like Romania or the L.A. riots on a bigger scale. I fear that deeply because we live and die by the gun so much in this country. In Czechoslovakia, it was a nonviolent change of power; same ultimately with South Africa. The reason those changeovers worked is that people who had been involved in very radical resistance movements knew there had to be a plan afterwards, even some loose idea of who should be doing what.

The time has come to start planning now, at least mentally, for what happens if there is a big takeover and the corporations fall. You don't want some horrendous dictatorship cooked up by multinationals and the Pentagon taking our current system's place. This whole thing could be accomplished democratically, but if there are going to be rock musicians and filmmakers in the legislature, like in Czechoslovakia, it had better be people with ideas and some knowledge and a network to implement them. It's time now to start thinking, "What do I do if I suddenly find myself in charge?" I don't think it's egocentric for everybody in this country to go beyond calling Clinton a sellout corporate a****** and start asking themselves, "What would I do in his shoes?" Take the hard issues, the Middle East, Bosnia, and how about giving everybody a place to live and a livelihood in this country; meaningful work is almost extinct in the land of life, liberty, and the pursuit of happiness. What are we going to do? Write down ideas. Bounce them off your friends. If you don't have intelligent enough friends, get new ones! Talk to your parents, your teachers. In some ways that sounds like jive, but I'm trying to find a better answer to that myself. It may take me my whole life, but this is what I've come up with so far. And above all, most of the people reading this aren't going to be radical activists or punk rockers forever, unfortunately, so it is important to learn from the mistakes of people who came before us, people we admire, like Tim Yohannan, and people we no longer admire, like '60s radicals who turned around and became right-wing cyber-yuppies. And don't let the attitude you have now evaporate if you start making money working for IBM. Always keep that with you and make sure it's passed down to your children. Don't give up and don't mellow out.

©2001 Punk Planet. From the book *We Owe You Nothing*, Daniel Sinker, editor, published by Akashic Books, Ltd. Used by permission.

4. Kathleen Hanna Interview (Excerpt)
Punk Planet 27, September/October 1998

Musician (Bikini Kill, Julia Ruin, Le Tigre), cofounder of the Riot Grrrl Movement

This interview was excerpted from We Owe You Nothing, *a collection of interviews originally published in the fanzine* Punk Planet. *In the interview,* Punk Planet's *publisher Daniel Sinker talks with Kathleen Hanna, cofounder of the band Bikini Kill and one of the originators of the Riot Grrrl movement of the early 1990s, which sought to introduce young women in the punk scene to feminist thought, to empower them to express themselves creatively, and to encourage girls to stake out a place for themselves in the male-dominated world of punk rock. During its heyday from the early to mid-1990s, Riot Grrrl received intense scrutiny from mainstream newspapers and magazines, with Hanna put forward as the leader of the movement. Eventually, she and others stopped talking to the mainstream press, and the publicity surrounding the movement faded. At the time of this interview, Bikini Kill had ceased to exist. Hanna was working on a new musical project, Julia Ruin, and had distanced herself from Riot Grrrl. She talks with Sinker about capitalism and feminism in punk and the role of art in America.*

Let's talk about capitalism in relation to Bikini Kill and Riot Grrrl for a second. Both of those phenomena caught an incredible amount of media attention. At a certain point, it seemed like all of you lost control of your own representation. It became larger than any of you and mutated into something really different. So now we're at a point where *Rolling Stone* declares last year as the "Year of the Woman ..."

So what is it now? Thanks for our year! I think it was Paula Poundstone or some other great female comedian who figured out that they told us it was the year of the woman when there were only three months left in the year—so really it was the three months of the woman!

What do you think went wrong there? Do you ever wish that things could have played themselves out differently?

I don't wish anything was different. If anything was different, I wouldn't be where I am and I wouldn't have the friends I have. I wish certain people hadn't died, but other than that, I don't have any big regrets.

As far as the mainstream media goes, when it first started happening, of course it felt really f***ed up. It's scary to see something that at one point in time was really important to you turned into a sound bite. But I still get a lot of really cool mail from girls all over the world, and that's definitely a result of the media attention.

When I was growing up, I didn't have access to fanzines. I didn't know about punk. Growing up in D.C., it seemed like most of the people who were into punk were private school people. The public school kids had no idea. We had feathered hair and were listening to Molly Hatchet. I can't change the fact that I didn't have access to it, so I don't want to be an a***** by saying, "You heard about it through *Rolling Stone*, so you're not really blah blah."

But it's gross when things like Riot Grrrl or feminism become a product. It's like, "Let's get it in as many magazines as possible so then everyone will know about it." I don't necessarily think that's the way to go about things because that's still reproducing a market economy. That's still saying, "Here are the managers that know the product that's best for you and you're just the stupid consumers that are supposed to consume it." Whether that product is feminism or that product is Colgate, as long as you're using those marketing concepts, you're still treating people like they're idiots and you're still reinforcing capitalism. I have a lot of mixed feelings about it. Do you remember the show Night Flight?

Yeah, they showed *Another State of Mind* like every three weeks.

Yeah! That's how I learned about punk. That was one of my main influences when I was younger. I didn't do anything about it for years, but I knew it was there and just knowing it was there made my life a little easier.

It's the never-ending argument about access to information. I'm stuck in the middle of that argument right now because of the bar code on the cover of *Punk Planet*.

I've had a similar problem. I was in this video. I was broke and I thought it would be fun because I wanted to see how major rock stars made rock videos. Anyway, I got two hundred bucks, which helped pay my rent. People were really p***ed off at me about it and said I was a big sellout.

I figured out who most of the people were who were p***ed and they were people who live at home with their parents and don't pay their own rent! I care what kids think, but it's a different thing when you're out in the world and you have to pay your bills. I'm not saying that I'm going to sell out to Sony. I'm just saying cut people some slack. If you're putting something nourishing out in the world, you have to nourish yourself too. Who gives a s***? Why is a bar code such a big deal? I don't see what the big deal is!

What if you work really hard to put out your fanzine and you spend a lot of time on the writing and you can't afford to give it away for free? What if you don't have a dad who has a secretary who will Xerox them all for you for free? If you spend all your money on printing a zine, you can't really afford to not get paid. Meanwhile, the kid who has the dad whose secretary Xeroxed them can go to a show and give them away for free. That could make you feel really f***ed up if you can't afford that. All I'm saying is that certain people can afford to be more generous than other people, and it's important to look at that.

In second-wave feminism, there was a similar problem. There's a lot of really good stuff in this book, *Daring to Be Bad*. There's this concept about how if you're successful, you're being "male," and I've always equated it with the punk thing of if you're trying to earn a living, you're being "capitalist." Both these arguments stem from the idea that power is always corrupt and that it's not possible for anybody to have any kind of power without being an a***** with it. That's a really pessimistic idea. It allows the oppressors to define what success is. I think there are a thousand variations on what success is. Why can't we take over the word "success" and have different forms of success that are about doing the things that make us really happy without sacrificing ourselves? Why is sacrificing yourself the highest order of the day in Western society? It's sick! I'm not saying that everybody should start businesses and become capitalists and f*** people over. It doesn't have to be like that. We can try to create alternative models for economic systems.

It scares me because I don't want to be reformist. I don't believe in reformism. I don't just want my piece of the pie. I believe in revolutionary action. I don't believe in trying to change the system as it is because the whole system has to change. In a way, I'm contradicting myself because I'm saying that we need to earn a living, but the ultimate goal is that we change the entire system. But unless we build models—even small little Lego ones in our houses—we're not going to figure out how that's going to come about.

If success means you're being "male" or being "capitalist," what does that leave us with? No dreams and nothing to strive for.

It's so frustrating because I say these things and yet I have met feminists where their whole thing is about getting ahead within the system the way it is. They're still defining success in the same way it's always been defined—by money and by how much control they can have over their environment. I'm really frustrated with feminism that doesn't have an analysis of capitalism, or anticapitalism that doesn't have a racial, feminist, or real class analysis.

In Yugoslavia, the workers owned all the means of production, but they still had to compete with each other because the people who were buying the products still wanted to buy the cheapest ones. There wasn't a rethinking of values, it was just a change from private-sector ownership to ownership by the workers. There wasn't a whole big challenge to the value system. The factories ended up competing with each other to a ridiculous degree. I see a similar thing in feminism.

If we don't challenge the unhealthy forms of competitiveness that capitalism breeds, or the way it teaches us to objectify ourselves and each other, then we're just selling ourselves out. Nothing's going to change. In Yugoslavia, they just changed who owned the means of production but they didn't change what was produced or how it was produced or the value system. With feminism it's the same thing. If you don't change the whole value system everywhere, if instead you say, "It's about white middle-class women getting an equal piece of the pie, too," then it's boring.

That's the grain of salt to take with my other argument that it is important for women to own businesses. We need to at least try to create new structures and new ways of dealing with things. But it doesn't have to be oppositional. It shouldn't be a choice between running a f***ed-up corporate business that doesn't think about what your products do out in the world, how your workers are treated, and why all the top management is from a certain group versus running a punk business, giving your products away for free, and having no structure. That just creates a whole new bogus thing where we're still defining ourselves in accordance with the Man because we're defining ourselves in opposition to him. We are contingent on him staying an a*****.

If you're in opposition to something, then you are in many ways lending it validity.

Totally. You're saying it's important enough to counter. My whole strategy is to say, "I don't even care." I mean, I'm not going to turn a blind eye while people are being murdered, but at the same time I'm not going to base my whole life on being the opposite of a bunch of necrophiliac a*****s. I'm going to try to create something that makes sense in the context of what's going on now.

What you're talking about is different than apathy, right?

I'm on this new trip of saying, "I'm an artist, dammit." I think that what I do is important enough that I should get paid for it. I'm not talking about getting paid a hell of a lot. I don't need a house in Malibu or wherever people get houses, but I don't feel bad making a little money off of what I love. I want everybody to be able to do that.

It seems really American to not respect the arts. I've been to Europe and they really respected artists and writers. It was important to them what food tasted like and what buildings looked like. They had squats with really good sound systems. It was so different than the United States. People there cared about food and art and literature. It wasn't a sidebar or a luxury for a certain class of people. It was recognized as an integral part of survival. Here, it's like you're supposed to feel guilty if you're an artist or a writer. You're supposed to not want to make any money off of it and feel really bad if you do.

You feel like you have to apologize for what you're doing.

Art is a job. It's just not a sucky job. It's important and it's valuable to the community. You should get paid for what you do. I'm really sick of the whole idea that art is this lazy thing that slackers do. I just visited this liberal arts school where a lot of the people there had this really oppositional view of art and activism. You either had to be an artist or an activist, there was no way that those two things could work together.

That's absurd! Art and activism have gone hand in hand for hundreds if not thousands of years. To insist that they're opposite is really denying a lot of history.

There are certain rallies that I want to go to, but I don't necessarily think that it's the place where I want to be political. All I've ever wanted to be since I was little was some kind of artist. I want to be a part of political activism and I want to be a part of the community, but I have to figure out how best to do that. I don't mean that I'm not going to do s*** work for people or for organizations that I believe in; it's just that I haven't found a community or a group that I want to be a part of in that respect. It's weird that people find art and activism to be a contradiction. It's as if the artist is supposed to be hedonistic and the activist is sacrificial.

Which is ridiculous, because you have to sacrifice so much to be an artist, a writer, a musician, or whatever.

But why is it an ideal to sacrifice at all? Why isn't it ideal to have a really good time while you're doing things? I think it's a joyous thing to fight back against oppression. I think it's all about saying, "I love life." Sometimes I hate life and it's a big-ass drag but I'm still having an interesting time being here. The whole idea of suffering sounds very Christian to me.

This weekend a friend of mine lent me some zines from her archive, including a copy of *Bikini Kill* Zine #2. On the cover of that issue it says "Girl Power." Later in the weekend it was my roommate's birthday and she wanted to go buy costume jewelry, so we went to the mall and Claire's Boutique was filled with things emblazoned with the words "Girl Power." I had this really strange feeling because I had just seen the cover of *BK* #2 and then saw all this stuff and I knew that this stuff had grown indirectly out of that. All I could keep thinking was how if this was weird to me, it must be unbelievably weird to you.

I remember when I first saw that stuff, I was really freaked out! [laughs]

How strange is it to maybe not have coined a term, but to have used it in one way and then eight years later turn on Spice World and see it stretched across Ginger Spice's breasts?

I wish I could have afforded that dress back in '91! It's really creepy to me. It seems like whenever anything has a chance to become radical in pop culture, they just get the Monkees to do it. They'll have auditions and get girls that won't say anything beyond "girl power!"

I know when I first started, I said things like, "It's really great to be beautiful and powerful and sexy," and I take a little bit of that back now. What I was saying was that you don't have to look a certain way or have a certain hairstyle to be a feminist; that just because a girl wears lipstick, that doesn't mean she's not a feminist. But now I realize that I wasn't really challenging the standards of beauty. A friend said to me, "Why is it so subversive to be beautiful in the traditional sense? I think it's much more subversive to create your own form of beauty and to set your own standards." She's right. I wasn't thinking about what I was saying.

The things that I was saying back then were very easily cooptable by capitalism and the mainstream media. They're very easily inter-preted to mean, "it's feminist to be really sexy for men." That's not what I meant at all! There are a lot of times when people think that in order to create something, you have to destroy something, and sometimes you do. Sometimes things have to be completely destroyed in order to change. But I don't think that in order to create a new happening or movement, people have to destroy what happened in the past. We need to build on the foundations that these past movements have provided. In my earlier days, I think I was doing things that were oppositional to history. I was drawing a caricature of old-school feminists. Even though I paid lip service to the feminism of the past, I don't think I knew my history like I do now.

I see it happening even now with younger women saying weird stuff to me that sets it up that I'm old school and they're new school. Now that it's happening to me, of course, I can realize how I've done that to other people and look back in my wise old age of twenty-nine and be glad that I'm not like that anymore. I think that old school and new school have a lot to offer each other—not that I consider myself old-school at this point anyway. I'm only twenty-nine!

The thing that could be possibly good or beneficial from the Spice Girls is that really little kids may be able to overlook the BS and get inspired by them. My friend Tammy's niece Crystal is staying with us right now and she loves the Spice Girls. She's this really amazing person and totally has her own thing going on and I think she's smart enough to make it into something that works for her instead of something she's working for. This other girl I know, Zoe, loves the Spice Girls, too, and she does these performances and dances based on them. I think she can turn it into something powerful. It can be cool if little girls are turning it into something that works for them or if people hear "girl power" and they want to know more about it, so they go to the library instead of going to the mall.

What really is girl power? It's when Angela Davis was put in prison and people went there and sang to her outside the window. It's these different moments when women really did seriously challenge the structure of society. That's girl power! My problem comes when it's just about barrettes and T-shirts.

©2001 *Punk Planet*. From the book *We Owe You Nothing*, Daniel Sinker, editor, published by Akashic Books, Ltd. Used by permission.

5. The Riot Grrrl Manifesto

Kathleen Hanna and her band Bikini Kill released the following statement in 1991 to summarize the reasons behind the Riot Grrrl movement.

A declaration by the band Bikini Kill outlining the Riot Grrrl philosophy:

BECAUSE us girls crave records and books and fanzines that speak to US that WE feel included in and can understand in our own ways.

BECAUSE we wanna make it easier for girls to see/hear each other's work so that we can share strategies and criticize-applaud each other.

BECAUSE we must take over the means of production in order to create our own moanings.

BECAUSE viewing our work as being connected to our girl-friends-politics-real lives is essential if we are gonna figure out how

[what] we are doing impacts, reflects, perpetuates, or DISRUPTS the status quo.

BECAUSE we recognize fantasies of Instant Macho Gun Revolution as impractical lies meant to keep us simply dreaming instead of becoming our dreams AND THUS seek to create revolution in our own lives every single day by envisioning and creating alternatives to the bulls*** christian capitalist way of doing things.

BECAUSE we want and need to encourage and be encouraged in the face of all our own insecurities, in the face of beergutboyrock that tells us we can't play our instruments, in the face of "authorities" who say our bands/zines/etc. are the worst in the U.S. and

BECAUSE we don't wanna assimilate to someone else's (boy) standards of what is or isn't.

BECAUSE we are unwilling to falter under claims that we are reactionary "reverse sexists" AND NOT THE TRUEPUNKROCK-SOULCRUSADERS THAT WE KNOW we really are.

BECAUSE we know that life is much more than physical survival and are patently aware that the punk rock "you can do anything" idea is crucial to the coming angry grrrl rock revolution that seeks to save the psychic and cultural lives of girls and women everywhere, according to their own terms, not ours.

BECAUSE we are interested in creating non-hierarchical ways of being AND making music, friends, and scenes based on communication + understanding, instead of competition + good/bad categorizations.

BECAUSE doing/reading/seeing/hearing cool things that validate and challenge us can help us gain the strength and sense of community that we need in order to figure out how bulls*** like racism, able-bodyism, ageism, speciesism, classism, thinism, sexism, anti-semitism and heterosexism figures in our own lives.

BECAUSE we see fostering and supporting girl scenes and girl artists of all kinds as integral to this process.

BECAUSE we hate capitalism in all its forms and see our main goal as sharing information and staying alive, instead of making profits or being cool according to traditional standards.

BECAUSE we are angry at a society that tells us Girl=Dumb, Girl=Bad, Girl=Weak.

BECAUSE we are unwilling to let our real and valid anger be diffused and/or turned against us via the internalization of sexism as witnessed in girl/girl jealousism and self-defeating girltype behaviors.

BECAUSE I believe with my wholeheartmindbody that girls constitute a revolutionary soul force that can, and will, change the world for real.[1]

NOTE

1. *Bikini Kill* (Olympia, WA), n.d., no. 2.

6. Cynthia Connolly

Photographer, artist

Cynthia Connolly was involved in the early Los Angeles punk scene before moving to Washington, D.C., in 1981. She wrote scene reports for Flipside *and worked for* Maximum Rocknroll *in the 1980s. She also worked off and on for Dischord Records for two decades. In the late 1980s, Connolly, Leslie Clague, and Sharon Cheslow collected photographs and anecdotes for* Banned in D.C., *their book about the punk underground scene in Washington, D.C., from 1979 to 1985. Connolly's photographs have been featured in numerous magazines and books and shown in art galleries across the United States. She has conducted workshops in Spain and New York City and at the Andy Warhol Museum of Art in Pittsburgh. In the following interview, which took place on January 17, 2009, Connolly talks about what initially attracted her to punk and the sense of community she found in the Washington, D.C., hardcore scene.*

You moved to Washington in 1981, but before that you lived in Los Angeles. Were you into the L.A. punk scene at all?

I grew up in L.A. In 1979 I saw these black and white photos in the *L.A. Times* of these bands in L.A. I grew up on the west side of L.A. where there were all these surfers and I hated the whole surfer dude culture because they were dudes. I wanted to surf but I immediately knew, "Oh, I'm a girl, I can't surf." I had grown up as a feminist but didn't know it.

I always wanted to be involved in a music or arts group that was more open-minded and where women were treated equally as men. I went to this exhibit on Russian avant-garde from the 1920s and it showed me that there are communities of people who were artists, and

I thought, "Why can't we have things like this now?" I wanted to find a group or community like that.

So when I saw the photos of those punk bands who were playing this new music, I wondered, "What is this? Maybe I should go figure this out." So I snuck out and took the bus to go see some bands and got involved in the punk music scene there before I moved to D.C. I listened to Rodney on the ROQ, which was great.

In L.A., it felt like a huge community of kids doing different things. Some were there for the music, some were doing drugs. I felt like I could contribute to something whether I was a girl or a boy. There was a community of kids involved in art and music, and it was mostly L.A. bands. By then they had already figured out how to create their own sound.

When I moved to D.C., there was a group of guys into music from England like the UK Subs and Stiff Little Fingers and it seemed like it was all about the music. It was mostly guys but I was into it because people were nice and it was a small community. It was cool that these kids who were 14 and 15 years old were recording. It was like one big family. In 1981, I met Alec and Ian MacKaye and John Falls—that's how I got involved with it. My attraction was to a larger community, hanging out, creating art. It was about the music and the culture, the movement, and it was so underground and weird because there was no radio. It was fascinating to be involved in it and experience it. I became more interested in the phenomenon of it than the actual music. How did all of the people all figure out that the show was happening? They would come from Philadelphia, New York, Boston, but there was very little advertising. Four months after I moved to D.C., it was obvious that something pretty interesting was happening. Then I thought that someone should take pictures, and I started taking pictures of things. I couldn't get good pictures because I had a crappy camera and a crappy flash, but that's where I started.

Did you consider yourself a punk?

Totally. I felt like I was breaking from this mold of what my mother came from where there was a role for the woman and a role for the man. And I felt that punk and our generation was going to change that. I still consider myself punk because I think in a different way, but the definition of punk is different for everyone. My definition of punk isn't the tough guys, the skinheads in the mosh pit—for me it's about doing what you want to do and believing in what you believe in. Standing by your ideas and actually pulling it off.

Were there many women involved in the scene at the time?

Well, it became less interesting to me as it became more masculine. I found it uncomfortable to be around the more violent aspect of things. But at the time, it was what was happening. In retrospect, a lot the music was white guys yelling, but it was what was happening. I was totally enveloped in the entire scene. It was really a movement that was a phenomenal experience. It was like catching a wave—you didn't really have to exert energy and you were just moved ahead in a group of people.

So for you it was not all about the music. It wasn't that you liked the bands and got into the scene that way?

I met the people and knew them directly and I liked their vision because it was like my vision. So I was involved with the scene because of this vision and the people who I thought were really great people. The music was an additional aspect. It was the glue that held it together for me because I thought there was something greater about it than just the music. I was in art school and people made fun of me and said, "Oh, art's not punk." Art was like an open field of creativity, and you could do whatever you wanted, and that's why it was hard for me to understand why someone into punk couldn't understand that.

I always felt that punk was so visual that artists and photographers played a huge part in its development.

Right. For the book *Banned in DC*, I wanted to do a book about the D.C. punk scene that expressed what was happening without being authoritarian and saying, "This is what was happening." That's why I included stories from people, so you get an overall feeling of what was happening.

I realized someone had to do a book on the D.C. punk scene because if we didn't, people would move away and the stories would be lost. And it had to be done on paper so it would last. I was about twenty-two and moved into my mom's house and started working on the book with

Leslie [Clague]. At first, people didn't realize we were doing this and didn't believe it because there were no books like this at the time.

I have a BFA in graphic design. This was before computers, so I wanted to do a nice book, but I didn't want people to think I was doing something fancy. It was still punk. But I wanted a book where the paper would last a long time. There was only one other punk book, *Hardcore California*, that wasn't on newsprint at the time. So I thought, "Wow can I do this so it doesn't look too nice but will be taken seriously?"

And then for a number of years you booked d.c. space (a small performance space)?

I wanted to buy an offset press and print zines, and I envisioned a coffeehouse with a printing press in the basement. Then d.c. space hired me because they thought I was organized. I ended up taking the job and did it for five years. I booked bands six nights a week, Monday–Saturday. What an amazing job—I couldn't believe it was my job! But the recession in the early 1990s was hard on d.c. space. The building was condemned because there was a problem with the sewer line and d.c. space couldn't afford to get it fixed.

When d.c. space closed, I worked for Dischord. I had already been working for them off and on for years, helping them out with stuff. I was hired in the fall of 1992 to do promotion for Dischord. Fugazi had started and they were growing really fast, so I was hired to do promotion for radio stations and fanzines. That went on for ten years, until 2002.

Thinking back, why do you think some people got into punk and others didn't?

I think it was different for everyone. For me, maybe I was just trying to find a community or another family, because my parents were divorced. I was looking for a group of people around me that was solid. Some of the other people who had good families were arty and into that side of it.

Did you see the punk scene as rebellious?

Yes, there was rebelliousness. In retrospect, maybe they were rebellious because they were trying to find something that was lost in their own lives. But the D.C. scene was so constructive and about creating a community. My mom always thought I was going through a phase, then she finally realized at some point it wasn't a phase anymore. But I think that every town's scene was different.

Do you think any of the remnants of the early punk culture have moved into mainstream American culture?

Now you can't even discern punk culture from the mainstream. So much of punk culture is enveloped in our American culture that it is our American culture.

7. Steve Pick Interview

Writer and cofounder of Jet Lag fanzine

A student in St. Louis, Missouri, in 1978, Steve Pick first heard punk music when a small college radio station began broadcasting a punk and new wave show. Drawn in by these new sounds, he became driven to know more about punk or, as it was being marketed as in those days, "new wave." Within a year, Pick had met and interviewed the Ramones, and he later cofounded the fanzine Jet Lag *to run the interview. The first issue's print run was 200 copies.* Jet Lag, *like hundreds of other zines created across the country, was produced by a group of people who wanted to inform the local community, as well as proselytize a bit and spread the word about punk rock. Until they found a national distributor, Pick and his partners sold the zine at shows, record stores, bookstores, and anywhere else that would carry it. Altogether, ninety-four issues of* Jet Lag *were published before it folded in 1991. By that time, 1,200 copies of each issue were being printed. Today Steve Pick is a freelance writer in St. Louis. He has a radio show and has written for the* St. Louis Post-Dispatch, *the* Riverfront Times, No Depression, *and assorted other publications. Although punk rock still permeates his blood, it is only one of his many musical interests. On December 16, 2008, Pick talked about what life was like for punk fans in the Midwest before and during the 1980s.*

You grew up in the Midwest, in St. Louis. How did you hear punk or find out what was going on?

It was a very small and very isolated situation back then. In my case, I came along in 1978, so I was a little behind the curve. And there were maybe seventy-five or a hundred people in town who were listening to punk before I was. There was one college radio station at Washington University, KWUR, which was ten watts, and you could barely pick it up where I was, ten miles away. Every Friday and Saturday night there were shows that played all of these new records, and that was my religious ritual—to listen to that and hear what was going on. It probably started in 1977, and I discovered it the next year.

Was there a club in town that would book punk bands?

No, at that time local bands would scramble around looking for places to play. They would play at private parties, and every once in a while they'd get booked into a club, but never on an organized basis. In 1979 this place called No Name Disco would have local bands every Monday night. That became a center, a place you would go because you knew everybody you knew was going because there was no other place to go. So it was really hard because there weren't very many shows. If you look on the calendars in *Jet Lag*, you can see there'd be about four or five shows in a month. That was it. It was really, really slow until about 1980, when there were more places to play.

How did your Ramones interview come about?

I originally planned to picket the local rock station, because they didn't play anything I liked. I wanted to convince them to play punk and new wave. I was interviewed about that in the paper by a local columnist, and I thought "I bet she'd like to interview the Ramones, and she could take me with her." She didn't want to do it but said she could get me the interview, so she set it up, which was an incredibly nice thing for her to do. So in November of 1979, three of us went. We walked into the hotel room and there they were—exactly as they look on their album covers. Afterwards, I gave the interview to a guy, Jim Roehm, who was publishing a free one-page sheet called *Noise*. But he had run out of money, so we took the interview back and put it out ourselves.

Some fanzines had a very specific focus, but *Jet Lag* has all types of stories. It's much broader than just punk or new wave.

If it had come out in 1978 when I first discovered punk, *Jet Lag* would have been much more narrow. But by 1980, I had two years of listening to different things, and everything I listened to led to something else. And all the other people writing for it were going through the same thing. We were all listening to different types of music, so we weren't trying to narrow it down. Albeit, we probably had arguments about it sometimes. I'm sure there were people involved who would say, "We're not going to write about The Who! Why would we do that?"

You have stories in one issue about 999, the Dickies, and Jan and Dean.

I definitely believed there was a history of rock that led to punk and new wave as its apex. We didn't really cover much heavy metal or Foreigner— the stories had to have some relation to what we considered rock and roll at the time. But that was constantly expanding.

You said that punk influenced your life, but it never was your life.

It was in a sense. I would have been going on through life without any idea that there was any path other than living in suburbia and going to work every day at some job I didn't like. It changed me from that and gave me this whole other set of options. Some people I meet who got into punk feel that what was set out in 1976 by the Sex Pistols and the Ramones is the be-all and end-all of punk. If music is loud and fast and aggressive, then it's good, automatically. What it did for me is show me one possible creative approach, and there are many, many others. So I kept trying to find out what all those other ones are.

What about the rebellious aspects of punk, questioning authority?

The whole nihilist aspect of what was going on didn't really affect me at all. To me it was more of a positive energy, so I experienced an opening of things rather than, "Let's smash things down." There was definitely an us-against-them feeling at the time. You could get beaten up just because you told someone that Led Zeppelin stunk. And there were times that I was threatened, although I was never actually beaten up. But I didn't feel I was actually rebelling against authority, but against any limits.

How were you able to get information before the Internet?

It's so different now. In the third or fourth issue of *Jet Lag* we wrote a Mitch Ryder obituary because somebody told us he was dead. Then I crossed it out on all the copies after they were printed and wrote "Ooops, he ain't dead." Back then we didn't have any way of confirming something like that. Now, instantly upon the death of a musician, there's a hundred stories online that you can find right away.

What does the term "punk culture" mean to you?

In the mid-1980s I went to a lot of hardcore shows, so I think of punk culture in two ways: the '70s punk culture and the '80s punk culture. The '80s punk culture was more of a teenage thing than the '70s culture felt like to me, even though I was a teenager in the '70s and not in the '80s. The bands in the '70s were older and in their twenties. In the '80s, a lot of the bands were 18, 19, 20, 21 years old. I think of the clothing and the openness and creativity and the experimentation.

Did the hardcore scene have the same feeling of openness and creativity to you?

Yes, it did. But at the same time, it was totally the opposite. I remember when Black Flag grew their hair out, how many arguments people had. It was the end of the world. There were people who just couldn't handle that. The music that was coming out was very creative and very open and helped to expand things beyond the way it seemed at first. The Meat Puppets' first album was just "aarrrrgggggg," really fast music and screaming. By the third album they were writing almost folksy kinds of songs. So I think it was definitely creative, but long-term it ended up with people demanding the more loud, fast, generic kind of music that came out in the '90s.

What did Black Flag growing out their hair mean to people?

It meant that they were hippies! They weren't true to the ideals of the scene as the kids understood it. If you look at it from the point of view of someone who was sixteen at the time and hearing something expressed that they'd never heard before, and then the people who were expressing it were moving on and doing something different, it was scary to them. Here's the first time someone's feeling connected to music in this way, and now it's changing on them. Most of the hardcore punks were somewhat isolated individuals until they got into that community, so most social networks or communities don't like change.

When you started *Jet Lag*, did you feel you needed to tell people about punk?

We really believed that the music we liked needed to be heard by everybody and then everybody would like it. I didn't understand why it was so controversial and why it couldn't be huge. But when I did start listening to hardcore, that was never the goal. I still loved it and wrote about it and wanted people to like it, but I knew that it could never be commercial, while the Ramones and the Clash should have been the biggest bands ever. I remember hearing the Cars on the radio and thinking, "Okay, we won! New wave is going to be huge." Instead just the Cars were huge.

8. The Ramones Interview
Jet Lag #1, March 1981

In the late 1970s, rock music had grown into a major industry as top bands sold millions of records and toured the world in private planes, stopping along the way to perform in sports arenas or stadiums for tens of thousands of fans. In contrast, punk operated in a small world where band members traveled by bus or van to play shows for hundreds of fans, and where even local kids could get the opportunity to talk to and hang out with their favorite bands. When the following interview took place in St. Louis in November 1979, the Ramones had released four albums and had recently recorded with legendary music producer Phil Spector. In their boldest bid for more mainstream success, they had also starred in the film Rock and Roll High School *and contributed songs to the soundtrack. The interview below appeared in the first issue of* Jet Lag, *one of the thousands of fanzines created, produced, and distributed by people in the punk community in the days before the Internet. From 1981 to 1991,* Jet Lag *kept St. Louis punk and new wave fans aware of what was going on in and around their city.*

On Nov. 26, 1979, the Ramones played a brilliant, loud set before a sold-out Mississippi Nights crowd. Before the show, the Ramones consented to an interview with your reporters, Steve Pick, George Dunn and Duwan Dunn which follows now.

Q: Your album with Phil Spector is coming out soon, right?

J: In February. February first.

Q: What are you planning to do after that? Are you gonna do another one with him?

J: It's hard to say. Possibly, you know.

Q: Your first three albums were interchangeable in a way. Then Road to Ruin came out and it was different, and the difference coincided with Marky joining the band. Was that coincidental?

M: The songs were written already.

J: So it was coincidental. We were planning on doing that for that album.

D: He added a different kind of beat, I think.

J: Yeah, maybe a little difference.

D: It was much better . . . it was a pretty big difference, really.

J: Each album we try to make a little different. I mean, you know . . .

D: We couldn't have had like most of those drum parts on it with Tommy in the group. There's no way!

J: Tommy had never played drums before until he joined the group and it was . . . made it a little more limiting.

Q: I read somewhere that when he joined he thought he'd help you more as a producer.

J: Yeah, I guess that's why he joined, you know. He didn't want to be a drummer.

D: That's what he imagined! That's what he fantasized!

J: He didn't want to be a drummer, you know, we just took him in.

D: He's just living out a dream, poor fellow! He didn't ruin the record, though. It came out real good despite everything. I really like it. It may have been the peak for us in a different type of way. You know, now we got something totally different to offer.

J: It really was . . .

D: It's not what I imagined.

J: . . . real powerful and fuller.

Q: Road to Ruin is a lot more serious than your other albums. Does that foreshadow a new direction for the Ramones? Will we hear more of that on the next album?

D: You know, when you're a songwriter, you know, you can look back on all the other songs and make a . . . like one big collective song out of it all, and that's probably what happened. The whole mood was like weird on the album. It's a very moody album. You know, it's like in writing the songs, we sorta knew more about what . . . what we could . . . the power of what we could say, you know, and how we could put it across. It was all real . . . nothing that . . .

J: There's only so many funny things you can sing about, you know.

Jo: This new album, it's very positive and it's very direct, you know.

D: That other album's like an exorcism for us, got a lot off everybody's chest.

Q: Were you trying to make a statement with it?

D: No, no that eludes me.

J: It's for people to interpret more than anything else.

D: I don't know . . .

J: It's for people to interpret and if they see a statement, you know, it's . . . an artist, you know, doesn't try to analyze his own work. It's just write the stuff and do it, you know, and it's what other people . . . whatever you see might be in it . . . in our unconscious mind, you know.

Q: I read someplace that you, Joey, had asked Bruce Springsteen to write a song for the Ramones. Has that happened?

Jo: I don't know. Well I was kidding, you know, because he was writing for Robert Gordon and everybody else. He might as well do it for us, too, you know.

Q: His best songs go to someone else.

Jo: Yeah, well he said himself that he doesn't like to do the ones that are most commercial. He'd rather take on a song that's more complicated and stuff. You know, but that's all 'cause he doesn't do as good . . . he doesn't do those songs very good anyway, you know. Like "Fire" . . . I thought that Robert Gordon did a better job.

Q: What kind of music do you listen to?

Jo: All kinds of music, you know. The Knack. (laughs)

Q: You like the Knack?

J: No, we always hated the Knack!

Jo: The Cars, Foreigner.

J: Ummm, everything, I mean, you know . . .

Q: Well do you listen to more punk stuff? Heavy metal?

J: We listen to that stuff. We listen to, uh . . . (sighs)

Q: Black Sabbath?

J: Occasionally.

Q: What was that business about you opening for Black Sabbath?

J: (pointing to Marky) He's got a Black Sabbath tape. We listen to it once in a while.

Q: I can understand that you may like them, but it seems that you're asking for it when you open for them.

J: I know! We didn't want to. It's just, uh . . .

D: You gotta learn from experience. That's what we learned.

J: They said you can't pass up the opportunity to play for ten, fifteen thousand people.

Q: What was it like?

D: It was hell!

J: It was terrible! It [sic] terrible!

D: Sometimes a big group will try and intentionally ruin your show, but Black Sabbath didn't pull those tricks. But it was still like . . .

J: They were nice but the fans were really . . .

Q: My little brothers are both hardcore Black Sabbath fans and they can't stand you.

D: What's wrong with those kids!?!

Q: I don't know.

J: I mean, like we liked Black Sabbath when they came out, you know whenever that was, ten years ago, but they didn't go . . .

Jo: Times change.

J: Times change and they didn't go anywhere, really, and it's still the same, and, you know . . .

Q: Led Zeppelin . . . they're all like that.

J: Everything was good when it came out! But I mean, I would think now the kids would need something of their own rather than something their older brothers and sisters had had, you know, that it's time for them to have something new.

Q: A lot of people are scared of anything new. They don't trust it.

J: Well usually young kids are more open-minded about things than the older people!

Q: Where I go to school people call me names because I like punk and new wave. The Editorials editor of our school paper wrote a horrible editorial on new wave.

J: Yeah, but that's what people wrote about rock'n'roll when rock-'n'roll started in 1956.

Q: But these are teenagers!!

J: You know they're being like old people were in 1956, you know
. . . that the other music is the old established music and that's
what it was like . . . the Patti Pages and Peggy Lees.

Q: We've been collecting petitions to get the local so-called "rock-
'n'roll" station, K-SHE, to play more new wave music like the
Ramones. Well about two hundred people signed, no problem, so
we called them up and they said they wouldn't even look at them.

J: Are any of them coming down to the show tonight, or what?

Q: I doubt it.

Jo: I listened to that station. It was horrible!

J: These stations, it's up to them to keep rock going and all they are
is bunch of old men playing music for old people. And they're not
thinking about kids or that, you know, if you have five hundred or
a thousand fans in a city, you deserve to be played, you know,
somewhat. You know, I mean, they're supposed to be the hip people, you know, and they're supposed to be looking into things like
that. All they care about is just business, you know! Play what
they're told to play! Puppets! They should go to the shows! The
radio stations should be going to every concert that comes to St.
Louis and check out how the people react to it.

Q: What's so dumb about the Ramones? Why do people call you
dumb?

Jo: Nothing's dumb about us, you know.

J: If you sing about something amusing, they think it's dumb, but if
you sing about the same thing that, like, Foreigner sings about,
that means you're smart. I mean, nothing could be more imbe-
cilic than, like, Foreigner.

Jo: They're trying to turn you off. Turn off all the people towards us
by saying that . . .

J: There I was slamming Foreigner.

Jo: . . . saying that we're lunatics or something like that. That we're,
you know, we don't compromise and do Toto songs or something
like that.

J: I mean, these people who call you dumb have to admit you're different and original. And to be different and original takes a lot more
intelligence than being the same. So if somebody says that you're
dumb, you know, you should ask them, well, do you find them different? You know, and let them answer that. And if they say

they're different, how can you be dumb and different? You're original.

Q: I have a pretty dumb question. About your pants.

J: That IS ridiculous! (laughs)

Q: Do you guys have your pants torn when you buy them or what?

J: No, no. See these are brand new. You just wear them during the daytime and you wear them for about a year in the day time and by next year I'll be able to wear them in St. Louis some night. (laughs)

Glossary of Punk Slang

Anarcho punk: A faction of the punk subculture (both bands and individuals) that promotes anarchist politics.

Bent edge: A term first used by Washington, D.C., punks in reaction to the straight-edge lifestyle, which called for punks to abstain from drugs, alcohol, and casual sex. Bent-edge punks were known for heavy drug and alcohol use.

CBGBs: The New York City club where the first American punk scene began in the mid-1970s. The Ramones, Patti Smith, Richard Hell and the Voidoids, Television, Suicide, the Heartbreakers, the Dead Boys, Talking Heads, and Blondie all built their reputations at CBGBs. In the 1980s, the club featured Sunday afternoon hardcore matinees that helped spawn another generation of New York punks that included Agnostic Front and the Cro-Mags. CBs, as it was widely known, closed in 2006, succumbing to pressure from rising rents in lower Manhattan.

Cowpunk: A subgenre of punk rock that began in and around Los Angeles in the 1980s when musicians combined punk rock with country, folk, and blues music in sound, subject matter, attitude, and style.

Crowd surfing: To be lifted up and passed around by the crowd at a concert.

Crust: Also called crustcore or crust punk, an extreme version of hardcore punk that arose in Great Britain in the mid-1980s, featuring lyrics that espoused anarchist political or social beliefs shouted or growled over extremely fast metal guitar riffs. A fan of the genre is called a **Crusty** and may be homeless or live in abandoned buildings.

Distro: A distribution source for independent publishing (e.g., zines), music labels, or software components (i.e., open-source components).

DIY (do-it-yourself): The essential punk philosophy or ethic of doing things yourself without relying on help from businesses, investors, or the mainstream media. DIY particularly relates to putting out music either on the Internet or on records and CDs, creating magazines and record labels, producing and promoting live shows, designing clothing, creating art, or making films.

Emo: Refers to bands that play music that is primarily "emotive" and features confessional lyrics and songs about relationships.

Goth: A punk subculture that began in the early 1980s. Bands such as Bauhaus and Siouxsie and the Banshees helped establish the gothic image as dark and depressing; goths wear primarily black clothing, often with touches of Victorian, Renaissance, and medieval styles and black makeup and hair. By the 1990s, the goth culture had expanded around the world and had splintered into many subgroups.

Gutter punk: Similar to a crusty, a punk who chooses to sleep on the streets, seldom bathes or changes clothes, and travels from city to city, occassionally with small groups of friends. Known for excessive alcohol and some drug use.

Hardcore: Loud, fast, and often angry punk music that arose in the late 1970s in Southern California and spread quickly throughout the country via Black Flag, Dead Kennedys, Bad Brains, Minor Threat, and others.

hXc: An abbreviation of "hardcore" referring to the music, scene, and people associated with it.

Indie: Short for "independent," used to refer to music released on independent record labels and outside the mainstream.

Liberty spikes: Punk hairstyle with gel or glue used to twist hair at the tip to form a "spike," creating a look that resembles the Statue of Liberty's spiked crown.

Mainstream: A term used in punk culture to describe anything that is widely accepted and commercially popular. Punks consider mainstream media, including music and movies, to be trendy and superficial.

Mohawk: A punk hairstyle, adopted from American Indian hairstyles, in which the sides of the head are shaved, leaving a two- to three-inch strip down the middle. Punks then add egg white, hairspray, soap, or glue to their hair to make it stand up straight.

Mosh pit: An area at a live show, usually in front of the stage, where people can jump around and bang into each other. The act of doing so is called **moshing.** See also slam dancing.

Old-school: Commonly used to refer to respected punks or bands from the 1970s or early 1980s.

Pit: Area at a live show where the audience can mosh and slam dance.

Pogo: A punk dance from the 1970s that consisted of jumping up and down in place. The Sex Pistols' Sid Vicious is often credited with originating this dance.

Pop punk: A term first used to describe punk music featuring pop melodies. The term was later used derisively to describe music created by people pretending to be punks.

Poseur: A person who pretends to be something they are not. This is an important concept in the punk community, for many punks value authenticity above all else.

Post-punk: The name given to bands from the late 1970s and early 1980s who followed the original punk bands by playing music that was more complex and introspective. The term was applied most often to British bands such as Joy Division, Gang of Four, the Fall, and the Cure.

Protopunk: A group of bands from the 1960s and 1970s that played with intensity yet limited musical virtuosity and who are credited with influencing the attitude and sound of punk rock. Garage bands of the mid-1960s, the Velvet Underground, MC5, the Stooges, and the New York Dolls have all been called protopunk.

Psychobilly: A combination of punk and rockabilly music popularized by bands such as the Cramps.

Queercore: A movement started by activists in the mid-1980s to highlight gays and lesbians within the punk community through zines that gave gay punks a forum, bands speaking out about gay issues, and festivals set up to highlight gay films, music, and bands.

Riot Grrrl: A politically motivated feminist movement that focused on gender equality in the punk scene. The movement began in the early 1990s and was popularized by the bands Bikini Kill and Bratmobile.

Scenester: People who follow some sort of music-related fashion trend such as goth or punk. Often considered a derogatory word, since many punks believe that scenesters value appearance above meaning or substance.

Ska punk: A combination of punk and ska (a rhythmic music from Jamaica) as played by bands such as Operation Ivy and the Mighty Mighty Bosstones.

Skanking: A type of punk and ska dancing in which the arms and legs are thrown around rhythmically.

Skate punk: A form of hardcore punk music developed by JFA, Big Boys, and others in the early 1980s. With its fast guitars, driving bass lines, and surf music–style drums, skate punk was popularized through the community of skateboarders who were fans of Southern California hardcore punk bands. Also referred to as skatecore or skate-thrash.

Skater: Someone who skateboards and is into punk music or a punk lifestyle.

Slam dance (slamming): An activity in which audience members at live music shows aggressively push or slam into each other. Slamming is often accompanied by stage diving and crowd surfing and is commonly associated with concerts by hardcore punk, heavy metal, and alternative rock and rock artists. Also known as "moshing."

Squats: Buildings where punks live, usually illegally, in a somewhat communal fashion.

Stage dive: When audience members climb on the stage and leap back into the audience while hoping the crowd catches them.

Straight edge: A movement within punk that eschews smoking, drinking alcohol, drug use, or casual sex. The term was coined by the band Minor Threat in its 1981 song "Straight Edge." The movement was popularized in the early 1980s by the bands SS Decontrol, 7 Seconds, Youth for Today, and others.

Zines: Pronounced *zeens*, these are homemade fanzines or magazines. Originally crudely drawn, typed, or hand-lettered and photocopied, zines were later printed or posted online. Most focus on music and political and social issues, but some discuss art, poetry, creative writing, cartoons, and other topics.

Annotated Bibliography

Books

Anderson, Mark, and Mark Jenkins. *Dance of Days*. New York: Soft Skull Press, 2001. An extensive look at the birth and development of the Washington, D.C., punk scene.

Azerrad, Michael. *Our Band Could Be Your Life*. Boston: Little, Brown and Company, 2001. Well-written and engagingly told tales of key bands in the hardcore and independent music world of the 1980s, including Black Flag, Minor Threat, the Minutemen, Hüsker Dü, the Replacements, Big Black, and others.

Blake, Mark, ed. *Punk—The Whole Story*. New York: DK, 2008. A collection of stories and photographs that originally appeared in three British music publications: *Mojo*, *Q*, and *Sounds*. Includes the editor's list of the seventy-seven greatest punk albums ever.

Blush, Steven. *American Hardcore, A Tribal History*. Los Angeles: Feral House, 2001. An in-depth guide to the American hardcore scenes across the country, a hardcore discography, and chapters on DIY, punk art, punk and the media, and why the hardcore scene ended.

Chernikowski, Stephanie, project coordinator. *Blank Generation Revisited: The Early Days of Punk Rock*. New York: Schirmer Books, 1997. A collection of photographs taken in New York City from 1973 to 1989 by top photographers in the punk scene, including Roberta Bayley, Bob Gruen, Ebet Roberts, and others.

Cogan, Brian. *Encyclopedia of Punk Music and Culture*. Westport, CT: Greenwood Press, 2006. Contains short entries, one to three paragraphs each, about everything punk.

Diehl, Matt. *My So-Called Punk*. New York: St. Martin's Griffin, 2007. A rare look at punk starting in 1994 with punk's commercial explosion and ending in 2005.

George-Warren, Holly. *Punk 365*. New York: Abrams, 2007. Despite a few questionable entries (Madonna?), this book contains 365 photos and short stories about well-known and not-so-well-known figures in punk.

Haenfler, Ross. *Straight Edge: Clean-Living Youth, Hardcore Punk, and Social Change*. New Brunswick, NJ: Rutgers University Press, 2006. A detailed academic analysis of the straight-edge movement, including a historical overview and chapters about positivity vs. militancy, women in straight edge, and life after straight edge.

Heylin, Clinton. *From the Velvets to the Voidoids*. New York: Penguin Books, 1993. Subtitled *A Pre-Punk History for a Post-Punk World*, this book focuses on the New York underground and punk music scenes from 1965 to 1980. Heylin relies predominantly on previously published interviews with members of the Velvet Underground, New York Dolls, and bands from the early CBGBs scene.

Leblanc, Lauraine. *Pretty in Punk: Girls' Gender Resistance in a Boys' Subculture*. New Brunswick, NJ: Rutgers University Press, 1999. The author, who was active in the punk scene as a teenager and now works as an academic and researcher, analyzes what attracts women to punk, how the punk subculture helps women define themselves, and how and why some women resist media and cultural messages about beauty and femininity.

McNeil, Legs, and Gillian McCain. *Please Kill Me*. New York: Penguin Books, 1996. An oral history featuring most of the major players from the early New York punk scene and a host of photographers, managers, friends, and lovers.

Monem, Nadine, ed. *Riot Grrrl: Revolution Girl Style Now!* London: Black Dog Publishing, 2007. Overview of the bands and the movement, including the British Riot Grrrls.

Mullen, Brendan, and Marc Spitz. *We Got the Neutron Bomb*. New York: Three Rivers Press, 2001. An oral history of the Los Angeles punk scene from the early 1970s' prepunk glitter days through the end of the Hollywood punk scene and the beginning of hardcore in 1981.

Nedorostek, Nathan, and Anthony Pappalardo. *Radio Silence: A Selected Visual History of American Hardcore Music*. New York: MTV Music, 2008. Examines private collections of materials—photographs, handmade T-shirts, rare records, letters, artwork—related to the hardcore scene from 1978 to 1993.

O'Hara, Craig. *The Philosophy of Punk: More Than Noise*. San Francisco: AK Press, 2001. A look at the philosophy and values found in punk and issues such as environmentalism, sexism, and anarchism as they relate to punk culture.

Pop, Iggy, with Anne Wehrer. *I Need More*. New York: Karz-Cohl Publishing, Inc., 1982. A brutally honest look at the life of one of rock music's few iconoclasts, as told by Iggy Pop himself.

Raha, Maria. *Cinderella's Big Score: Women of the Punk and Indie Underground*. Emeryville, CA: Seal Press, 2005. A well-researched and well-written look at female musicians in punk from Patti Smith to Peaches. Contains a discography, extensive endnotes, and a bibliography.

Sabin, Roger. *Punk Rock: So What?* New York: Routledge, 1999. A collection of essays from cultural critics that assess punk's place in the history of popular culture, primarily from a British perspective.

Savage, Jon. *England's Dreaming*. New York: MacMillan, 2002. Originally written in 1991, this is one of the definitive books on the Sex Pistols and British punk. It also contains information about early American punk and a number of minor, yet interesting, figures who played a role in punk's development. Revised in 2002 to include the Sex Pistols' reunion.

Sinker, Daniel, ed. *We Owe You Nothing: Punk Planet—The Collected Interviews*. New York: Akashic Books, 2001. A collection of lengthy and thoughtful interviews originally published in the well-respected fanzine, *Punk Planet*. Contains well-known punk spokesmen such as Ian MacKaye, Jello Biafra, and Steve Albini, along with lesser known figures such as Duncan Barlow and Los Crudos.

Stark, James. *Punk '77*. San Francisco: RE/Search Publications, 2006. An oral history about the 1976 to 1979 San Francisco punk scene featuring interviews with V. Vale (publisher of the *Search and Destroy* fanzine), Ness Aquino (owner of the famed punk club the Mabuhay Gardens), and members of the Nuns, the Avengers, Crime, and the Dils.

Taormino, Tristan, and Karen Green, eds. *Girl's Guide to Taking Over the World: Writings From the Girl Zine Revolution*. New York: St. Martin's Griffin, 1997. Contains essays about sex, self-help, entertainment, drugs, and food from zines published by women. Includes interviews with some of the zine publishers and a directory of zines.

Turcotte, Bryan Ray, and Christopher T. Miller. *F***ed up and Photocopied*. Corte Madera, CA: Gingko Press, 1999. A collection of flyers used by punk bands to promote their shows from 1977 to 1985. A historical record that captures the art and energy of the times.

Turcotte, Bryan Ray. *Punk Is Dead, Punk Is Everything*. Corte Madera, CA: Gingko Press, 2007. A look at the visual side of punk through flyers, fashions, set lists, and posters. Includes guest writers from the punk scene, along with interviews.

Films (Documentaries)

1991: The Year Punk Broke, directed by David Markey, 1992. Showcases a group of American punk and alternative rock bands touring Europe in 1991, including Sonic Youth, the Ramones, Nirvana, Dinosaur, Jr., and Babes in Toyland.

American Hardcore, directed by Paul Rachman, written by Steven Blush, 2007. A look at the hardcore movement from 1978 to 1985, as the filmmakers interview key people in the scenes from Southern California, Washington, D.C., Boston, New York, San Francisco, and elsewhere about what attracted them to hardcore.

Another State of Mind, directed by Adam Small and Peter Stuart, 1984. This film follows a self-planned and self-promoted 1982 U.S./Canadian tour by California bands Youth Brigade and Social Distortion. The film offers an interesting look at punks in various cities and the difficulties the bands faced as they put the DIY philosophy into practice.

Decline of Western Civilization, Part 1, directed by Penelope Spheeris, 1981. Takes the viewer into the world of Los Angeles punk just as the Hollywood scene was dying out and the hardcore was taking off. Contains interviews with the Germs' Darby Crash and Black Flag and performances by X, Fear, and others.

D.O.A., directed by Lech Kowalski, 1980. Follows the Sex Pistols on their ill-fated 1978 U.S. tour that culminated in their final show in San Francisco and their breakup.

End of the Century: Story of the Ramones, directed by Jim Fields and Michael Gramaglia, 2003. An insightful, heartfelt, and at times disturbing documentary about the dysfunctional faux family called the Ramones.

Punk Attitude, directed by Don Letts, 2005. Provides a quick-moving history of punk, from the Velvet Underground in the mid-1960s to Blink-182, circa 2004. Representatives from most of the influential bands, from the MC5 to the Clash and Bad Brains, weigh in about the importance of punk as a movement.

Punk's Not Dead, directed by Susan Dynner, 2007. An engaging look at the state of punk in the new millennium through interviews with many of the major figures in punk, including the large number of British punk bands from the late 1970s that have remained together for three decades.

Films (Features)

Class of 1984, directed by Mark Lester, 1982. This gritty, low-budget film about a group of punks that terrorize a high school plays up the caricatures of punks prevalent in mainstream media in the early 1980s.

Repo Man, directed by Alex Cox, 1984. A surrealist satire set in Southern California, starring Emilio Estevez as Otto, a young punk hired to repossess cars. The film pokes fun at cults, televised religion, punk criminals, UFO believers, the CIA, generic food, and other segments of modern American life.

Smithereens, directed by Susan Seidelman, 1982. A young girl comes to the big city looking for fame in this independent film. Shot on the streets of lower Manhattan, it aptly captures the noise, dirt, and feel of New York City circa 1980. Stars punk icon Richard Hell as . . . a punk icon.

Suburbia, directed by Penelope Spheeris, 1984. A widely praised film about punks who escape families where they are abused or ignored by living together in abandoned tract houses in Los Angeles. Spheeris' decision to cast young people she met at punk shows or in clubs gives the film an air of authenticity.

What We Do Is Secret, directed by Roger Grossman, 2007. A biopic of famed Los Angeles punk band the Germs and their charismatic lead singer, Darby Crash. With the help of former Germ Pat Smear, the producers worked hard to recreate the Germs' chaotic, violent performances and the Los Angeles punk scene as it was in the late 1970s.

Fanzines

The Book of Zines. www.zinebook.com. A Web site for all things zine (archives, reviews, and history).

Flipside. www.flipsidefanzine.com. A memorial site for the *Flipside* fanzine, with a database of early issues.

Maximum Rocknroll. www.maximumrocknroll.com. Online home for the long-running fanzine.

Operation Phoenix Records. www.operationphoenixrecords.com/archivespage.html. A punk zine archive with back issues of *Maximum Rocknroll, Flipside, Suburban Voice, Heartattack,* and *10 Things Jesus Wants You to Know.*

Profane Existence. www.profaneexistence.org. An independent media cooperative that includes both print and online editions of *Profane Existence* magazines.

Punk magazine. www.punkmagazine.com. Home of the resuscitated *Punk* magazine.

Suburban Voice Online. http://subvox.blogspot.com. A blog written by *Suburban Voice* publisher, Al Quint.

Web Sites

924 Gilman. www.924gilman.org. Home page for the 924 Gilman Street Project, an all-ages, nonprofit, collectively organized music and performance venue in Berkeley, California. Includes information about how to volunteer, a schedule of upcoming shows, and band flyers and videos.

ABC No Rio. www.abcnorio.org. Web site for the ABC No Rio center for art and activism in New York City. Includes a schedule for upcoming Saturday hardcore matinees.

Mr. Roboto Project. http://therobotoproject.org. Site for the all-ages cooperatively run performance space in Wilkinsburg, Pennsylvania. Includes event listings and information about getting booked to play there.

Punk Voter. www.punkvoter.com. Seeks to inform and engage millions of punk fans in political action.

Punkbands.com. www.punkbands.com. An independent Web site maintained by fans. Includes album reviews, interviews, news, and articles about punk and topics that may interest punks.

Punknews.org. www.punknews.org. An all-volunteer staff updates this site daily with news, reviews, tour information, and interviews related to punk, ska, hardcore, emo, metal, and indie music.

Search and Destroy. www.trashsurfin.de. A punk rock and roll search engine.

Index

About the Author

SHARON M. HANNON is a freelance writer who has written about topics ranging from women explorers to World War II, spies and secret agents, and the American Revolution for clients such as the Library of Congress and the Public Broadcasting System (PBS). She first became interested in punk in high school after buying records by the Stooges and the New York Dolls, followed by the first albums from Patti Smith, the Ramones, and the Sex Pistols. Early in her career, she wrote concert and record reviews for local papers. Music has always been, and remains, a part of her daily life.